Authentic (*adjective*): true or genuine; real; not a copy or a reproduction; not false or imitation.

Personal (*adjective*): particular to a given individual; of or arising from personality; "personal magnetism."

Style (*noun*): the way in which something is done or expressed; a manner of expression characteristic of a particular person; distinctive elegance; a way of handling elements or forms that gives identity to a particular person.

THE LOOK

A Guide to Dressing from the Inside Out

RANDOLPH DUKE

Clarkson Potter/Publishers

NEW YORK

To my close women friends,

women I have dressed,

women I have never

known and have

only seen in pictures, and

the thousands of women I have

met in my career who have inspired

me to write this book and show them

the beautiful possibilities inside of them.

acknow

There are so many important people who helped make this book possible:

All the women who opened their lives, hearts, homes, and closets to me and the camera to help us illustrate points in the book: Merle Ginsberg, Claudia Grau, Shawn King, Marilyn Lue, Tamara Mellon, Cheryl Tiegs, Tobi Tobin, Constance White, and Erinn Williams. Ladies, I could not have done this without you!

I especially thank Sandra Graham, whose true beauty (both inner and outer) not only graces some of the pages ahead but blesses my life on a daily basis. She has been my steadfast soul mate for nearly two decades, and not a day goes by that I don't thank God for bringing her into my life.

My dear friend Richard Pollmann, who has seen me at my best and worst, and has always stood by me. He is without doubt the definition of true friendship . . . unconditional, honest, and always there.

My dear friend Bruce Kaye has been a source of inspiration for nearly half of my life. Bruce has supported me through thick and thin. No matter the ups or downs, Bruce has been the loyal friend one can only dream of having. His gifts are many, and I thank him for sharing them.

To the wonderful writer Karen Kelly, who so beautifully translated my philosophies, concepts, and ideas into the written word, I give special thanks. Her insight and enthusiasm has made this book not only possible but a very rewarding and memorable experience for me as well. I could not have done it without her.

Andrew Matusik, for his tireless patience, hard work, and great eye in taking the photographs for this book. Thank you to Caroline Bergonzi for the graceful illustrations and cover styling.

Tobi Britton's expertise with makeup and hair were priceless additions

ledgments

to the New York photo shoots. Paige Padgett worked her makeup and hair magic at the Los Angeles shoots.

The actresses and recording artists I have had the privilege of dressing: Edie Falco, Barbra Streisand, Amber Tamblyn, Joan Allen, Sharon Stone, Marcia Gay Harden, Helen Hunt, Thora Birch, Daisy Fuentes, Rebecca Gayheart, Julie Moran, Leann Rimes, Carrie-Ann Moss, Jennifer Lopez, Debra Messing, Ellen Burstyn, Kim Cattrall, Angie Harmon, Jane Leeves, Kate Driver, Sarah McLachlan, Allison Janney, Kate Capshaw, Hilary Swank, Ming Na, Garcelle Beauvais, Jennifer Love Hewitt, Charlize Theron, Courtney Thorne-Smith, Britney Spears, Mary J. Blige, Jada Pinkett Smith, Faith Hill, Kristen Johnston, Jennifer Aniston, Lorraine Bracco, Angelina Jolie, Celine Dion, Rebecca Romijn, Heidi Klum, Mira Sorvino, Minnie Driver, Jill Hennessy, Rita Wilson, Kim Basinger, Lisa Kudrow, Geena Davis, Laura Linney, Geri Ryan, Illeana Douglas, Kim Delaney, Tyra Banks, Calista Flockhart, Lara Flynn Boyle, Felicity Huffman, Kelly Clarkson, Kelly Preston, Virginia Madsen, and Laura San Giacomo.

Rachel Witte, June Saltzman, and Marty Neelan of HSN, for giving me the chance to bring my designs to so many different kinds of women.

Clarkson Potter and Aliza Fogelson, for giving me the opportunity to bring my message to a large audience.

The stylists, makeup artists, hairstylists, and photographers I have worked with over the years have been a constant source of inspirational creativity.

And finally, I thank my muse . . . my mother, Dagny Garner, whose beauty undoubtedly influenced my path, and whose pride has taken me years to finally realize and appreciate. I do feel loved.

contents

foreword

Randolph and I have been friends for more than twenty years. We met in 1985 when I walked into the Randolph Duke store in New York City. The clothes were like nothing I had seen anywhere else—modern, architectural, many of them with transformative features that gave them a great deal of versatility. More important, when I tried them on it was obvious that this designer knew a woman's body. He knew how to design clothing that made a woman feel as wonderful as she looked.

Upon meeting Randolph I immediately realized that he understood the insecurities and fears women have about their bodies . . . how we feel in the dressing room when the door is closed and we look in that mirror! In part it's because of his early professional years designing swimsuits, but it goes further than creativity. I find him very intuitive: he empathizes with the difficulties we have selecting clothes we like that also make us look and feel great.

Customer evolved into friend and fashion confidante, and eventually Randolph and I began working together. We opened his first wholesale showroom in 1985 and continued through the relaunch of the Halston brand along with its twenty-three licensees. Randolph has created gowns for numerous Hollywood actresses, including Angelina Jolie, Jennifer Lopez, Kim Basinger, Geena Davis, Jennifer Aniston, and Hilary Swank. Minnie Driver was the first, and I still remember him sketching the idea for her Academy Awards gown on a napkin.

No matter where his career has taken him, Randolph has remained committed to creating clothes that make a woman look and feel beautiful. Fashion has taken us a lot of places over the past twenty years but now has settled into a wonderful place of freedom--a place where any woman, regardless of age, income, or figure, has the opportunity to express her own personal style. In *The Look*, Randolph shares his knowledge and experience to show all of us how to use this freedom to our own advantage. Style is anything but superficial. It starts on the inside with the confidence and self-assuredness you feel when you know you are at your best. *The Look* shows you how to develop and present your true style. It's like having Randolph right there alongside you every step of the way. Enjoy!

—Sandra Graham,
jewelry style director of eBay and
owner of SJB Vintage & Couture

"Know, first, who you are, and then adorn yourself accordingly."

—Epictetus, Greek philosopher

CHAPTER 1

reclaim your style

The fashion dilemma nowadays is that anything goes. How do you know what's right for you when *every* fashion rule has been thrown away? If I were writing this book in the 1950s, it would be so much easier. Postwar prosperity and conformist gender roles (Mom at home, Dad at work, 2.5 children at school) led to convention in the closet, too: slim suits, midcalf hemlines, and muted colors dominated daytime wear. For evening, full-circle skirts bolstered by layers of tulle, tight and often strapless bodices, and an emphasis on the waistline or bust were standard. And pants for women? I don't think so! At least not in public. In the postwar era, very few women broke free of the socially prescribed uniform. Fashion was predictable back then, but that made it safe and uncomplicated.

ABOVE LEFT Fifties fashion was uptight in more ways than one!

BELOW In the '60s, fun, freedom, social consciousness, and politics came together in the fashions of the times.

ABOVE RIGHT Angelina Jolie in Randolph Duke. Today, movie star style influences everyone from fashion editors to soccer moms.

In the 1960s, the mood changed drastically, and fashion went through a truly revolutionary transformation. Many of you probably have fond memories of your first pair of hip-huggers, or going braless under a peasant blouse. Hey, it was easy then, too. Maybe you were in high school or college, excited about the wider world; perhaps you even took part in the youth movement. Dressing in a certain way became part of your social consciousness. Even if you missed the '60s or '70s, you certainly know about them. Nothing's been the same since.

Youth culture, street fashion, and multiculturalism became very influential on Seventh Avenue during those years and they continue to be. Celebrities, movie stars, and musicians also inspire many of the trends that filter down into department stores. Think about how far we've come: for the first time in the history of fashion, it's impossible to define a universally accepted style, pinpoint a required hemline length, identify a color trend, or clarify a day or a nighttime look. As a result, many of you are left pondering confusing choices, and in the process have lost touch with what you really like—especially those of you who have traveled the fashion road from the '70s and '80s to the '90s. Final destination: the twenty-first century. The ride you've been on, commandeered by capricious fashion gurus, the media, and manufacturers, has been a long and bumpy one.

That's why I can't blame you if you've thrown up your hands and resigned yourself—unhappily—to a lifetime of sweatpants, T-shirts, and sneakers. Many of the savviest style mavens I know are perplexed by the mixed style messages they receive every day from an ever-proliferating array of sources. Tweed jackets, pencil skirts, micro minis, granny skirts, big shirts, tiny Ts, midriff tops, sweater shrugs, drop waists, high waists—stop!

This sea change in fashion—from the dictatorial to the ironic (mixing high with low, such as a dressy embroidered jacket worn with faded jeans and strappy sandals), from personal to multidirectional (such as vintage pieces paired with modern ones)—parallels what's happening in the wider culture. And it's not a coincidence. You now have the freedom to customize your lives down to the smallest detail, from programming your television schedule with TiVo, to burning your own music CDs, to posting political or personal commentary on your own Web site, to serving Chinese takeout at a formal dinner party! But self-determination can be both confounding *and* exciting, especially when it comes to fashion. Being your own expert isn't a simple matter when it comes to your clothes.

We are so out of touch with what we really love, and seeing too many images of perfection has eroded our confidence. Hence the cliché of the woman throwing open her closet full of clothes and exclaiming, "I've got nothing to wear!" To me that reaction comes from not being happy with yourself. It happens to me, too. When I look in my drawers or my closet and I hate everything, it's usually because I am not feeling good about myself . . . and when I feel great, I love everything I have and it's easy to get dressed. But I know myself well, and I understand what looks good on me and what I love wearing. And since I'm a man, the options are more limited. The fashion business is primarily directed at women, and all that fashion "noise" can get very loud.

I also think women have more of a tendency to put themselves through the inadequacy ringer than men do. When you don't feel good about yourself, you go back to picking on yourself about things you don't like. Stop playing the ugly tape now!

Why? Because there is a way to get your confidence back and your closet in sync with your psyche. The current fashion landscape offers an opportunity to find and cultivate your own personal style—a style that makes you happy and has you looking your best. It's energizing and exciting to finally be able to shape your own ideas and interests into a unique style statement. Boundless choices and a no-more-rules attitude present a tremendous opportunity for you to find and wear what you like. How? It's easier than you think, but requires time, an open mind, and a willingness to play.

The Look is for every woman who is frustrated by today's fashion messages and choices. More important, it shows you how to define and express your individual style to take best advantage of your assets. This book answers your enduring wish to look beautiful, strong, sexy, feminine, and fashionable, right here, right now.

The trouble with the style advice found in many books and magazines is the approach they take. Most of the time the guidance boils down to show-

> ## "Style is what makes you different."
>
> —C. Z. Guest,
> socialite, gardener, and author

ing the latest styles on impossibly thin models airbrushed to perfection within an inch of their lives. It's tough to do more than that when new products constantly need to be assessed, vetted, and presented to readers. Fashion publications, working on tight deadlines, don't have the time to answer questions like "How do I develop my own look?" and "How do I make the current styles part of my own unique style?" Women end up feeling as if the fashion is imposed on them; instead they should be imposing *themselves* on the clothes! That's what *The Look* helps you do. It takes you on a journey that, ultimately, reveals what's been hidden, maybe for a very long time.

What Is Authentic Personal Style?

Great style transcends fashion. Think about great women of style; they don't conform to what's hot or trendy. Their elegance comes together bit by bit, using the process of an artist. The result reflects their inner being and their physicality. An iconic example of personal style, Katharine Hepburn created a look that was a very authentic reflection of who she was. It was not a formal look. She was a very pragmatic and direct woman, and her clothes were, too. She would not wear overly elaborate, fussy styles—that was the antithesis of who she was. And the clothes she chose suited her shape.

Diane Keaton has a very heightened and extremely idiosyncratic personal style. She wears gloves for no other reason than she likes to. Sarah Jessica Parker chooses to be eclectic; Gwen Stefani is a fashion adventurer—she's in the fashion vanguard. Madonna has done every look. None of these women slavishly follow the dictates of fashion. On the contrary, fashion makers look to such women for inspiration.

None of these women, or any other woman with great personal flair, was born with personal style or developed it overnight. Just like you are doing now, they figured out what silhouettes looked best on their shapes, got to know what they loved, and translated this knowledge into a way of dressing. They put their personal stamp on every outfit by putting it together through fearless trial and error—everyone has to try new things and make mistakes, at least in the beginning—until they arrived at a look that's truly their own.

Authentic personal style comes from understanding our bodies, recognizing the demands of our particular lifestyle, mining our experiences for inspiration, and finding what we really like. It's not something you can get simply from flipping through magazines and looking at pictures (although that can certainly help you get started). Style authenticity starts with confidence. It's about setting your own agenda and dressing and living fearlessly. Making yourself happy is at the root of it all. Women who have unique fashion flair are originals. There are no stylists hovering in the background.

The Look teaches you the secrets of how to unearth your personal style and become an active participant in your wardrobe. It shows you how to use your own ideas and preferences to build a wardrobe that flatters your figure, pleases you, and is consistent with the demands your life makes on you. I systematically demonstrate how to become *your own* image consultant, stylist, and fashion guru. Remember: there is no such thing as an "ordinary" woman, only ordinary clothes.

Sometimes personal style manifests through one look (e.g., romantic, classic, or bohemian); sometimes it unfolds through many different looks. Finding and celebrating your personal style is not the same thing as feeling pressure to create one defining look and to stick with it forever. It's being aware of what you like and conscious of how your clothes reflect that. Eventually, expressing yourself through dressing becomes second nature.

Are you a less-is-more or a more-is-more woman? Both are fine, if you know how to put your preference together in a way that works with your figure, not against it. There are so many benefits to getting in touch with your style sense. When you start expressing yourself through your clothes, you look better—and who doesn't want that? And all of a sudden you want to start making other changes: you feel brave enough to ask for a raise, organize your house, get rid of things that are holding you back, or approach that adorable guy on the subway platform. I've seen it happen.

The Look is not a makeover book. I do not dictate what you should wear because "the designer knows best." I don't know best—because I don't know you. So how could I possibly tell you what to wear? Unfortunately, I can't be there with you when you are shopping or getting dressed. So better I teach you how to put together your own look, on your own. The old chestnut "Give a man a fish and he eats for a day; teach him how to fish and he eats for a lifetime" holds true for getting dressed. A stylist could put together a look for you, and you would be dressed for a day. Know how to do it yourself and you'll look great forever.

At any rate, there's something about the idea of a "makeover" that bothers me. The word implies that you don't know what's good for you, but designer X or TV host Y *does*. You have to give yourself over to someone else, who tells you what to do, whether you like what they say or not. I don't buy it.

It's not that women don't have a personal style, it's that you've all been convinced by outsiders not to trust your instincts. *Everyone* has a personal style—after all, we have preferences in everything from food to friends. Clothes, color, cut, and fit are part of life, too.

I have confidence that your instincts about what you like and what you don't like are right on. The dictatorial approach isn't me, anyway. All you need is some information about the how's and why's of fit and style, and to open yourself to self-discovery, and you can be in love with your closet again. There is one rule: if you aren't having fun with your clothes—if you don't enjoy wearing what you have—you are wearing the wrong things!

You may also get stuck because you don't fully understand what your figure offers you and what the fit and the clothes can do for it. Once you have that information, you are off to the races.

Style Is Within Your Reach

The good news is you can uncover, rediscover, and cultivate what you love most about clothes. For those of you who have been wearing one style for ages and feel it's not "you" anymore, you're probably right and you, too, can make the leap, get rid of the old style, and find a new one that reflects who you are today. That's the secret about personal style—it's not static and it does and should change. If you have been wearing the same look for a decade or more, it's going to be scary to change—but also thrilling.

After all, you're not the same person you were five, ten, fifteen, or twenty years ago, right? So why should you dress the same as you did back then (or even the way you dressed yesterday)? It's not just about making sure your wardrobe keeps up with changes in fashion. It's about keeping up with yourself. Just because something is said to be "in" doesn't mean you have to

19

RECLAIM YOUR STYLE

wear it or that it's right for you. Once you have established your personal style, you can add all the fun, trendy pieces you like. And since there is so much out there today, there is no reason you can't find something in a style you love, that expresses your desires, and that's also up to the minute. Once you find your personal style and allow it to evolve, you never look or feel dated.

I've organized *The Look* in a naturally progressive fashion. First, my Shape of Style system shows you how to identify your figure type. Before you can do anything else, you must know your body. That information allows you to choose the right silhouettes for your figure—it's the cut and the fit of clothes, not the particular style, that flatters and balances your figure. The chapters are overlapping layers of information—so it's better to work through them from beginning to end than to start in the middle.

Experimentation, exercises, creative projects, and journaling also get you closer to where you want to be. Those are found throughout the book, under the Style Diary headings. The exercises in the book are not intended as literal instructions on how to develop personal style, or dictates on how to dress. Far from it. They are helpful tools you can use to access all the facets of who you are and stretch your creativity (and maybe stretch the boundaries of what you think about style and clothes).

Finding your "fashion voice" is possible only when you push your imagination past comfortable boundaries. And you have to make a little mischief and have a little fun, too.

I help you stock your wardrobe with essential layers and then use them to dress for your intention (work, play, seduction . . .). I also show you how you can use accessories; separates, hair, and makeup advance your personal style intentions.

Once you know how to use my system, you can *always* use it. It works independently of current trends. That means whether you're a working woman, a downtown diva, a soccer mom, a country girl, or a city slicker dying to break out of your fashion rut, you can get in touch with your secret stylish selves!

Then we explore how using a single personality piece helps turn an outfit into a true original. Finally, we clean out your closet and then go shopping.

You'll also meet an amazing group of women along the way, ladies who exemplify true authentic personal style. Together we see how they put together their looks. I think you'll find it very inspiring.

The Look is about you—it's not about me. I have many strong opinions about, well, everything. And I share some of them with you—along with tools and information that help you define and express your style. But ultimately, should it really matter what I or anyone else thinks about the way you dress? No. Unless it really matters to you and your intention is to always please other people. But it's much more important to please yourself. You can and should experience just how much fun getting dressed can be every day. It's an aspect of life any woman, anywhere, and at any age can enjoy. So, let's get started!

Start the Journey

Gather up a pad, a pen, and maybe a couple of fashion or celebrity magazines. Find a comfortable chair, pour a glass of wine or make a pot of tea, and settle in for thirty minutes or so of private time.

Jot down everything you hope to accomplish by discovering your style voice and revamping your wardrobe. Include fashion fantasies and dreams—all of them. For example, have you always wanted to be an alluring vamp à la Charlize Theron? Write it down. Do you lust after the rock star style of Sheryl Crow? Put it on paper! Have you always wanted to explore a sexy look that Beyoncé would envy? Make a list of every kind of look or piece of clothing you've fantasized about wearing— from classic to totally outlandish.

If pictures from magazines describe these things better than words, use images instead. Think about and then make a note of the things that may be holding you back from discovering your true style. What on the list can you change right now? What can you work with or around? Which ones are really just baseless fears—can you cross them off the list completely? If you can, do so.

Take another look at your list when you have finished this book. You'll see what you have accomplished and even how you may have changed from this initial foray into self-discovery. Prepare to be pleasantly surprised.

style diary

"The body is a sacred garment."

—Martha Graham, choreographer

what it offers you. Women who have great
style don't all have perfect figures, but
they do have one thing in common: an
intimate knowledge of their body
and a clear understanding of
what looks good on it. This
knowledge lets stylish women
select and wear clothes that
accentuate their positive features and minimize the aspects
of their figures they don't love so
much. This, in turn, allows them the
freedom and confidence to express their
personality through clothes. When dressing,
you can use the art of illusion to enhance your
best features and create an aura of beauty—and it's
not such a big mystery if you understand your shape.

The good news is that once you know your shape, you can wear *any* look you love—modern, classic, sophisticated, eclectic—if the elements are cut to suit your shape! As you'll learn in the subsequent chapters, if you really love modern-style clothes, for example, you can wear them as long as you select the right silhouette. Think about it: these days you can walk into any department store or boutique and choose a black trouser that is high cut, low rise, or hip hugging, with pant legs that are cropped, ankle length, or longer, and pegged, straight, boot cut, or wide legged. One of those styles is right for you, and after going through the exercises in this chapter and the next one, you'll be able to choose the pair of black pants that flatters your figure. But I'm getting ahead of myself.

It's so important to identify your shape right off the bat, before you begin to assess what you own, define and expand your style, or even go shopping. Once you know exactly what you have to work with, you'll be able to select the right cut and fit of any style of clothing that appeals to you.

Getting to know your body is scary, I realize. That's why it is absolutely crucial to confront anxieties about your body by taking the emotion out of the process. The positive feelings tied to what you like in terms of style, color, and texture come later. My system, the Shape of Style, is an easy and objective (I like to call it clinical) way for you to categorize your body type so that you can find the styles you love in the silhouettes that flatter and enhance your figure. *Rather than limiting women, the Shape of Style opens doors.* Every body is unique, but I have boiled down the most common shapes into five categories; I'm sure you can see yourself in one of them.

The five types are general enough to account for differences in height and bone structure but specific enough to be useful. I have purposely made each name plainly descriptive—no fancy or funny names here to conjure up a judgment or a value. The shapes don't imply anything other than that's what you have to work with. No one shape is really "better" than another. Every woman, no matter what her figure type, can look beautiful in clothes. This is not the time to say, "My hips are too big" or "My shoulders are too narrow." Your hips are your hips, and your shoulders, your shoulders. They aren't "wrong"; they are what you have and you can use them to your advantage.

My Shape of Style system helps women overcome their fears and shows them that they can look great in any kind of clothing, as long as it is made to suit their shape. I'll lead you through this process, and show you how to behold your body with appreciation and love.

Part of the assessment process is making peace with what you've got. That doesn't mean giving up or resigning yourself to living with qualities you can change, hide, or alter. It means saying, "I have wide hips; let me figure out how to dress to make them appear in balance with the rest of my body." I never say "never." I advocate all of it—from shoulder pads to falsies to plastic surgery, *if* it fulfills your desires. That's a big *if*, though. I recommend seeing what you can do with clothes first, before you add on anything or take away extras. It's amazing what you can create with the right silhouettes.

Besides, even if you do end up losing weight, your basic shape usually remains the same and you end up gravitating toward the same silhouettes. However, if you experience a particularly dramatic weight loss, say 30 or 50 pounds or more, you should reevaluate your body type, if only to celebrate your accomplishment and, of course, to check if you've gone from middle figured to linear or another shape.

I have worked with so many different kinds of figures, first as a swimwear designer, then as a New York–based fashion designer, and later in Hollywood, on films and for individual actresses and singers. Film and TV distort how people look. The cut and fit of clothes is even more important when you are being photographed, and I know every trick in the book. The secrets of illusion dressing are available to everyone, and it all starts with the figure.

The Shape of Style

In twenty-five-plus years of designing swimwear, separates, and evening gowns for women of all shapes and sizes, I have come to recognize five archetypical shapes, which I see again and again. Whether you are tall or short, thin or zaftig, have thin or thick ankles, large or small upper arms, you fall into one of these general categories, and knowing which one helps enormously in selecting the right silhouettes to put on your body. Some of you may experience instant recognition when you look at the icons or read the following descriptions. But hold on. Let's take a moment to do the visual "paper bag" assessment described below. You may surprise yourself and come up with something different than you assumed.

style icons

The linear-figured woman's bust, waist, and hip dimensions all measure about the same. Often a linear woman has a small bust and narrow hips, which makes her waist appear wider or more in line with her upper and lower torso. Long legs contribute to a linear appearance, but ladies with shorter legs can also be linear figured if the torso is straight. A linear-figured woman is athletic or thin. Gabrielle Reese, Teri Hatcher, and Nicole Kidman are superb examples of this shape.

THE HOURGLASS

The hourglass woman's bust, shoulders, and hips or shoulders and hips are noticeably broader than her waist. (If your waist appears just slightly smaller, you are more likely linear figured.) The hourglass creates a highly symmetrical curved line, making such figures pleasing to the eye. An hourglass woman has a lot of options to change the appearance of her figure if she so desires. Salma Hayek and Halle Berry are gorgeous examples of the hourglass woman.

The middle-figured woman is full figured and broader at the waist, or her waist, top, and bottom have the same circumferences. She may have a large bust and hips, but the middle curve is her defining feature. Short legs emphasize the middle, but women with long legs can still be middle figured. Queen Latifah is a stunningly beautiful example of a middle-figured woman.

The lower-figured woman is widest in the lower portion of her torso. She can be super-curvy and even busty and still be lower figured if her hips and derriere are wider than her bust or shoulders. In the past, this figure was called "pear-shaped," a term I absolutely loathe. It has a negative connotation, and at any rate, who wants to think of herself as a fruit? Lower-figured women are sexy and can emphasize their backsides or not as mood allows, à la Jennifer Lopez.

The upper-figured woman has wide shoulders and/or a large bust and a narrower waist and hips. Often she has a small waist and curvy hips, but either her shoulders are very broad or her bust is ample enough that the visual emphasis remains on her upper torso. The size of her arms is not the key here: it's the upper torso that does the talking. Angelina Jolie and Dolly Parton are sultry, sexy examples of upper-figured women.

Paper Bag Self-Assessment

Do your paper bag assessment when you have some time—on a lazy Sunday or when the kids are out of the house. Do it when you are feeling well rested (don't do it after a long, bad day at work!). Don't skip this step—it helps you so much when selecting clothes to serve different purposes. Something you think is a flaw may actually be an asset or become one with the right clothes. If you know what you have, you can use it to your advantage.

The first thing you need to do is take off your clothes. That's right. Everything. If you feel uncomfortable (or cold), put on a one-piece bathing suit, a simple and well-fitting bra and panties, or a bodysuit or workout leotard, if you have one. But it's really better to be stark raving . . . naked.

Next, take a clean paper bag and cut out two holes for your eyes. Objectifying your body is one of the simplest and most accurate ways to assess it. Put the paper bag over your head. Suddenly it's as if the body you are looking at is someone else's. You are no longer "you." Your personality, the glint in your eye, your smile, even self-esteem and feelings (often so apparent in our expression) are hidden and you are simply looking at a body. You can be so much more objective about what's there once you can't see your face and the look on it!

While being objective, remain positive about what you see. Remember not to judge! Just record your observations. Later on, we can carry this same idea of looking at yourself objectively into the dressing room. It's a handy way of seeing the outfit and not the person—you—wearing it.

Even though we are removing the emotion somewhat from the process by covering your face, this can still be a very emotional process. That's why it is so important to neutralize it as much as possible—and the

Personal Paper Bag Self-Assessment

Note that I refer to every one of your features as an "asset." There are no "flaws" in the Shape of Style system. At any rate, an asset by definition is not only a "benefit" but also a "quality," something you own and use to your advantage.

ASSET	DESCRIPTION
NECK	_____
SHOULDERS	_____
BUST	_____
WAIST	_____
STOMACH	_____
HIPS	_____
LEGS (general)	_____
THIGHS	_____
CALVES	_____
ANKLES	_____
HANDS	_____
FEET	_____

MY SILHOUETTE IS: _____

_____

_____

_____

_____

_____

paper bag is sort of funny, but it really helps. For some of you this may be the first time you have really looked at your body and assessed it. Some of you may not have done so in a very long time. But don't be afraid—this important step will help you find your authentic style. Go slow. Relax. Giggle.

As you look in the mirror and turn slowly, make note of what you observe—and evaluate honestly. Is your torso long or short? How does your upper torso compare to your waist and lower torso? Is the overall shape of your torso curved, straight, or rounded? If you have defined curves, are they most defined on the top or bottom? Are your breasts high and small? Large and round? Widely set or close together? Are your shoulders broad or narrow? Is your belly soft and gently rounded or flat?

Turn sideways and examine your profile. How's your posture? Is it straight or somewhat curved? What about your behind? Look at your backside. What does your torso look like from the back?

Are your legs long or short? Are your calves long and lean or muscular and rounded? What about your ankles—are they thin or thick? Are the backs of your arms soft or firm? While the legs and arms are not defining features of your overall Shape of Style, make note of them. If you have great legs, you can draw attention to them while distracting from a small bust or a wide middle. If you would rather not show off your upper arms, there are ways of camouflaging them while still dressing for your body shape.

I predict that your Shape of Style is becoming very clear. Can you see now that you are lower figured or upper figured? Maybe you are angular or hourglass. But you're seeing it now, and that's the important thing.

Use a pen and a pad or the form on page 33 and describe what you see.

reflection
perfection

It's important to invest in a couple of full-length mirrors, which can be easily found at hardware or home improvement stores for very little money. Attach them to closet doors or mount them on a wall in a corner (one on each side). It is so important to see what you look like from every angle: head to toe, front to back, and side-to-side. Not just for this exercise—but every time you get dressed. You're always coming and going; the world sees you from all sides.

posture perfect

I always think of my mother as taller than she really is because she has a presence. It's also because of the way she carries herself. She was a dancer and a Las Vegas showgirl, so she has posture *down*. She holds herself beautifully to this day.

Dancers know that good posture really does make you look longer, leaner, slimmer, and more graceful. The clothes you wear look, fit, and drape better when you are standing up straight. Posture is not only important for the way you look in clothes; it's good for your self-esteem. When you stand up straight, and your back is aligned, you begin to feel taller and more confident. You even walk differently—with more purpose and elegance. Your carriage is important in maintaining back health, too. That's especially true as we get older. Good posture is an instant antiaging remedy.

Not sure how to stand up straight? It's easy. Stand against a wall and pull your shoulders back so that both your shoulders and your behind are touching the wall. Put your chin slightly up and straighten your neck. Now slip your hand into the space between the wall and your lower back. If you are standing properly, your hand should touch both the wall and your back. If it doesn't, tilt your hips slightly back so it does. Then walk straight away from the wall. This is good posture. You may have to practice this move (why not every morning, before you get dressed?), but before long, perfect posture becomes instinctive and effortless.

The Big Cover-up

Whether you are linear or middle figured, you can have thick ankles or less-than-sculpted upper arms. An hourglass and a lower-figured woman could both have thin calves. Nobody's perfect, and there are certain features that can be minimized with little difficulty. Here's a quick guide to designers' tricks of the trade for diminishing the most common imperfections, no matter what your Shape of Style (no plastic surgery required!).

Short in stature (under 5′5″): Monochromatic color schemes from top to bottom create a long, uninterrupted line. For example, if you are an hourglass and a belted trouser suits you, choose a belt color that blends with your pants and top instead of one in a contrasting color. If you are middle figured, stick to tonal tops and bottoms.

Heavy arms: Long-sleeved shirts that taper down to the wrist create a slim line, as do raglan sleeves (where the seam is on top and runs down the side of the entire sleeve, instead of being fitted around the armhole). Cuff detail and bangle bracelets draw the eye down to your wrists. Jackets and other tops that have slim vertical lines, like long narrow lapels, minimize heavy upper arms. Sleeveless and cap-sleeved tops maximize heavy upper arms, as do tightly fitting jersey sleeves. If you go sleeveless, grab a lightweight pashmina to drape around your shoulders and cover the upper arms.

Skinny arms: Gently gathered sleeves and tops with dropped shoulder seams conceal superthin arms. Cap sleeves add visual weight as well. Sleeveless tops emphasize thinness. The drape of a shawl made from a fluid fabric conceals the tops of your arms.

Short legs: Monochromatic bottom elements create an uninterrupted line. That means pants or skirt, belt (if applicable), shoes, and trouser socks or hose should be in a similar tone. Short-legged women can wear skirts no shorter than 2 or 3 inches above the knee for maximum affect. Any shorter and your legs look truncated. A midcalf or ankle-length skirt works if it is right for your overall Shape of Style, in which case look for one that skims the hips in an A-line for the sleekest vertical. Pants worn with similarly colored pumps are a short-legged girl's best friend, because they create the smoothest, longest vertical.

Thick ankles: When wearing skirts, choose hose and shoes in the same tone to create a slim vertical line. Avoid shoes with ankle straps—instead try shoes with a deep front V and little ornamentation. High-heeled sandals should be slip-ons or have a back or heel strap, not a front strap, even if it goes across the top of your foot. This type of shoe draws attention to the ankle. Boots are fantastic with pants. Simple loafer-style flats also work with slacks; pair them with knee-high trouser socks of the same tone as the pants and shoes. Avoid ankle socks or any shoe style that draws a circle around your ankle in any way.

Mirror, Mirror

Okay. You've looked at yourself in front of a full-length mirror—naked or nearly so. Even with a mask on, I know that it was difficult to be honest and objective, without being overly critical about your shape. But you did it. Accomplishing a self-assessment is a huge achievement and you should be proud! Congratulations.

Now sit down and write a love letter to your own body. Yes, a love letter! And it's really important that you do this, even if you think it sounds corny. Include no negatives! Express only positive and loving thoughts about your body. If you find it impossible to say anything redeeming about your shape— which I doubt—then *thank* your body for what it has done for you. For example, express gratitude to the legs that have supported you and taken you where you needed to go, and the hips that cradled and gave birth to your children, for example. Then commit to your body as it is, make peace with it, and agree to work with what you've got to achieve your best results. You can't defer your style to some moment when you are "perfect."

Finally, make a list of what you really love about your body. Here's a sample list:

Great hands

Long neck

Cute behind

Nice knees

Once you have identified your favorite features, you can dress to enhance, accentuate, and play them up. And as an added bonus, when you do that, you are also minimizing those features you aren't so in love with.

_____

_____

_____

_____

_____

_____

"Fashion is architecture: it is a matter of proportions."

—Coco Chanel

CHAPTER 3

dressing details

Identifying your Shape of Style figure
type is the first step on your way to defining and cultivating your personal style. As
I've said, the most stylish women know
exactly what they are dealing with and
are able to choose the right shapes
for their figure. That means they
can eliminate certain things
off the bat, often innately.
They also know when to say,
"The hell with rules, I'm wearing this because I love it." *That's*
authentic personal style. Maybe
you're not at that stage yet. You're still
getting to know the basic Shape of Style
Silhouettes guidelines, and the layers of
dressing that make them up, but don't worry, you
are on your way there. The more you practice with
pieces that flatter your figure, the easier it becomes
to take calculated risks and creative chances.

Style Silhouettes for Your Shape

The right clothing silhouettes visually bring your figure into balance and proportion. A properly chosen skirt, a trouser of a certain cut, a T with a twist make all the difference in how you look. The right cut of clothing lets you use the art of illusion to your best advantage, and best of all, with the right silhouettes you can express authentic personal style freely and still look fabulous.

The hourglass is the archetypal figure because it is balanced and in proportion. The hourglass shape, therefore, is the basic figure that most women want to achieve. The symmetrical curves of the hourglass are pleasing to the eye.

Luckily, the right cut can create lines where there aren't any and diminish curves where you, well, don't want them to be. The Shape of Style guide to silhouettes helps you to visually create an hourglass, if you wish, and emphasize and further flatter the hourglass if that's your shape. But you can certainly choose clothes to emphasize your shoulders, bust, or bottom, too, if that's your desire. If you want to look lower figured or upper figured or linear figured for a certain purpose, you can create those illusions with clothes!

The Shape of Style Silhouettes are *general* guidelines about which shapes work best with which figure types to bring your figure into proportion. From there you can dress any way you like. Use this chapter as an interactive tool, because you can't really just *talk* style—you *have* to try the clothes on to see how they look in three dimensions on your body. So you're going to have to open your closet or visit your favorite store and start playing around with the shapes to see exactly what I'm talking about. That's part of the fun.

Select the Best

Figure-flattering silhouettes magically change your appearance. They create a pleasing line that is flattering to everyone. In fact, take the time to try on the shapes that I *don't* recommend. You'll see clearly why they don't work as well for your shape—but you may find some interesting exceptions.

lingerie: the second skin

Your clothes depend on your undergarments to make them look good. An incorrect or badly fitting bra can make the right top seem all wrong. Ditto for panties— a bad pair can put a wrinkle in your outfit by creating unwanted bulges and lines.

To prevent underwear slipups, make sure bras fit properly. Try them on instead of just grabbing the size you think you are. It's even better if you can visit a lingerie shop or a department store that offers full customer service. A trained pro measures you and then finds and fits you for the correct size. Comfort is key: straps should not cut, the band should not ride up your back, and closures should come together without strain. Underwires should sit comfortably under your breasts. To avert a bad decision when buying a bra, be sure to try it on with the kind of clothes you wear over it. A lacy bra, for instance, looks like a mass of bumps and wrinkles under a tight T. That's probably not the look you're going for. Better to stick with a seamless underwire or support style in that case.

Your lingerie drawer should hold a few styles of bras and panties for different wardrobe functions. How many bras you need comes down to how many different kinds of clothes you really wear. If you go to a lot of formal events, you need bras that support you underneath evening gowns with low or no backs or plunging necklines. A convertible bra lets you rearrange the straps so you can wear it as a regular two-strap bra, a halter, or a strapless. That makes it very versatile. If you have full breasts, you want to go with something that has a lot of support. If not, you can find many different and comfortable padded styles these days that really help balance your figure.

> "Brevity is the soul of lingerie."
>
> —Dorothy Parker,
> novelist and poet

Panties should be smooth, finely knit, and comfortable. A cotton crotch is preferable, even on the tiniest G-string. Elastic around the waist and legs should not dig into you; and lines should not show through clothes. Bikinis, high-cut briefs, and thongs create the most seamless coverage with maximum comfort. I'm not a big fan of boy-cut styles and tap-pants (i.e., little satin shorts). They don't seem particularly comfortable worn under clothing, and they don't work well under pants or skirts because they have a tendency to show their lines and pucker up. But if you like 'em, wear them "as is" around the house. Sexy! Control panties are great when you require more support on the bottom. The point about panties is that they should be comfortable and invisible under clothing.

37

layers of dressing

the essential

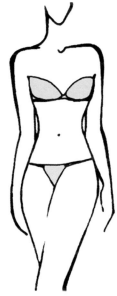
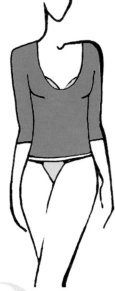

The secret skin.
This is the layer that gives comfort next to your body and support for the garments you present to the world. Consisting of bra, slip, undershirt, panties, or stockings, your secret skin provides the foundation for your silhouette. The secret skin should also make you feel fabulous and sexy.

The second skin.
A camisole or a shell, this element of attire, while sometimes optional, is the first layer you present to the world. Often it's basic in fabric and style and can offer a flash of color or an interesting texture, serve as a backdrop to a necklace, or provide a contrast to the "personality piece."

The essential top.
A sweater, a blouse, a shirt, or a jacket (or a dress that is part of the "essential bottom"), this garment organizes and presents the entire top portion of your torso. It should give you the shape, cut, color, pattern, and energy that best suits your body, your personality, and the intention you want to fulfill. Sometimes the essential top can be your personality piece.

Whatever silhouettes are right for you, there are seven essential layers (six if you are wearing a dress) when getting dressed, whether it's for "casual Friday," Saturday shopping, or opening night at the opera.

Putting together a look is easier when you break it down into steps. Simply being conscious of what you're wearing leads to greater clarity about your personal style, especially as you consider the fit, function, color, and intention of each piece.

In this chapter we'll take a look at the Shape of Style Silhouette specifics of the first four layers and of the last, the protective envelope. The finishing touches and personality piece are so important that they have their own chapters (see chapters 8 and 9 for more details).

The basic bottom.
A skirt or pants work with the essential top to give your body the form you want to present. Usually these items are neutrals that make you look curvaceous and sleek so that your lower body acts like a pedestal that presents the upper portion of your body. The basic bottom balances the upper proportions by continuing the desired line.

The personality piece.
Whether it's a velvet jacket, a snakeskin belt, a faux fur poncho, a sexy pair of shoes, or an outrageous turquoise ring, this element is your outfit's personal signature. The personality piece defines your mood, your intention, and, more than anything else, your personal style.

The finishing touches.
Accessories are fundamental to a complete outfit. A bracelet, a necklace, a brooch, or a purse, and your fragrance, makeup, and hair, while subtle details, unify your outfit and give it a finished look.

The protective envelope. This optional layer is great when chill winds blow or when the snow flies—après pool or après ski. It's your coat, jacket, shawl, or wrap.

linear figured

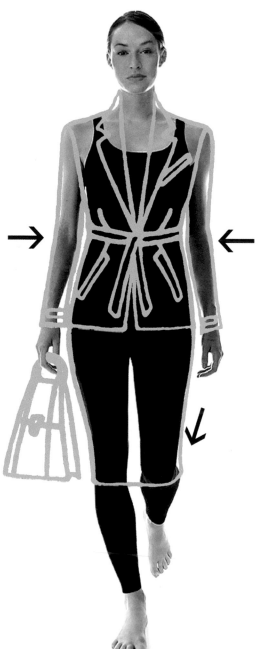

THE SECOND SKIN
Knit Jerseys, Tanks, and T-shirts
To flatter, try V- and scoop necks, or a fitted top with a boatneck, which creates a horizontal line. Think twice about tops that are cut straight on the side seams, or long, straight tunics.

THE ESSENTIAL TOP
Blouses and Shirts
Fitted and tailored shirts with contrast-color details (i.e., piping, stitching, front-patch pockets, or horizontal lines) create curves and angles. Shoulder pads and decorative embellishments at the shoulder create the illusion of width on top. Think twice about boxy, straight, and tunic styles as well as sleeveless tops that are deeply cut— they further narrow your upper torso and shoulders, emphasizing the vertical line.

THE ESSENTIAL TOP
Jackets and Blazers
Look for fitted jackets that cinch at the waist and flare at the hips. A fitted jacket that ends at the waist can help break up straight lines. Safari and belted jackets also work well. Think twice about boxy jackets that are either tunic length or hip length.

THE BASIC BOTTOM
Skirts
You can wear most any style, as long as it has a waistline: A-line, bias, wrap, pegged or pencil, flared or circle, and dirndl or gathered skirts all create curves. Think twice about straight skirts with no waistband, especially those that are very long, unless you want to emphasize your angularity.

Pants

Tailored waist-high pants with pleats and cuffs work well, and Capris create a curve from your waist. Boot-cut pants with a slightly dropped waist also create curves. Pegged or ankle-length pants create movement. Think twice about straight pants with no waistband.

Dresses

A belted dress creates the illusion of a waist, as do wrap dresses; bias-cut and fit-and-flare styles also work. Think twice about boxy or straight-cut styles, horizontal lines or stitching, and clingy knit dresses that emphasize your straighter lines.

Coats

Trench, belted, and tailored coats, and flared or fit-and-flare styles create curves. Think twice about balmacaans (loose, full overcoats with raglan sleeves commonly made from twill, wool, or canvas) or straight-cut coats. Swing coats can make the linear woman look off balance.

Combine light tones with light tones and dark tones with dark tones in complimentary colors on top and bottom to create the illusion of curves. For example, in autumn, a V-neck burgundy cashmere jersey worn with tailored and pleated forest green slacks defines the top, bottom, and middle of your figure and makes it appear as if you have an hourglass shape. In summer, a cream skirt with a celery-colored T-shirt does the same thing.

the hourglass

Knit Jerseys, Tanks, and T-shirts

To flatter, try anything fitted. V-necks, scoops, and U-necks and flared or fitted sleeves are pretty. Think twice about cap sleeves (if your shoulders are broad), cropped tops, and tube tops.

Blouses and Shirts

Fitted and tailored shirts, peasant-style tops, and tunics work beautifully. Think twice about tops that are severely cropped or very loose and baggy.

Jackets and Blazers

Choose fitted blazers that skim the hips and accentuate curves, and belted safari jackets that reach the hips. Think twice about boxy shapes and jackets that end at the waist, which cut you in half and shorten your torso.

Skirts

A-line, wrap, pencil, and bias styles are smart choices. A wide waistband is great if you want to accentuate a small waist. Think twice about boxy minis, short pleated skirts, or dropped waistlines.

Pants

To flatter, classic man-tailored trousers with a fitted waist and boot-cut pants work well. Wide waistbands, placket fronts, and pleats are pretty possibilities. Slightly flared pants flatter by creating length and enhancing your natural curves. Think twice about pegged pants and Capri pants, which cut your lower leg in half.

Dresses

Try wraps, fitted shifts, and belted shirtdresses. Think twice about loose-fitting styles, muumuus, Empire waists, and horizontal lines.

Coats

Try A-lines, wraps, trenches, and fitted coats with belts. Think twice about swing coats and dolman-sleeved balmacaans (loose, full overcoats with raglan sleeves commonly made from twill, wool, or canvas), which hide and distort your shape instead of showing it off.

COLOR WATCH

Hourglass figures have few color caveats. Monochromatic schemes create a long line. Depending on your size and height, you can try different combinations of lights and darks. Short women are better off with light on top and dark on bottom, which creates a long leg. Tall women can shorten their legs by doing the reverse, but why would you want to do that?

middle figured

Knit Jerseys, Tanks, and T-shirts

U-shaped necks and scoop necks frame and emphasize the face, V-necks elongate. Boatnecks broaden your shoulders if they are narrow and bring your figure into balance. Try untucked styles that skim gently over the waist and end at the top of the hip line or that are mid-hip length. Watch out for oversized styles, which make you look bigger. Think twice about jerseys and Ts that require tucking in. Tucking creates a line around your middle and draws attention to it.

Blouses and Shirts

To compliment your body type, try untucked styles with a finished (not shirttail) hem that extends past the waistline and hits the top of your hip. Think twice about very tailored blouses or shirts that require tucking. A straight hem can be left out—a shirttail usually needs tucking. Avoid wrap styles with a waist tie, which emphasizes the waist.

Jackets and Blazers

Semifitted or straight-cut styles that reach the hips and cover your behind create a nice line. If you're short, it's best not to go much longer than the top of your thigh with a jacket. A one-button style is most flattering because it creates the deepest V, which elongates and slims your middle. Think twice about belted jackets, cropped styles (especially those that end at your tummy), wide collars (they visually extend your middle), and flap or large patch pockets (they emphasize your middle).

Skirts

Consider bias-cut and A-line styles with a flat front. Look for a skirt that does not have a waistband. Avoid pencil skirts, pleats, side or front-patch pockets, and trouser-style zipper fronts.

Pants

Flat-front, straight, and bootleg cuts create a nice curve. If you have a flat behind, try tighter, fitted styles with back pockets. Think twice about side pockets, pleats, and high-cut waists. Pegged-leg pants emphasize a wide waist. Capris cut and shorten the line of your leg.

Dresses

A dress that skims the waistline is most becoming. A coatdress, an A-line dress, an Empire or high waist, or a slightly fitted shift with bust darts and a V- or scoop neck is pretty. A dress with matching coat is also an option. Avoid dresses with a belt (especially one in a contrasting color), wrap dresses, or very fitted dresses.

Coats

To flatter, try an easy-fitting balmacaan (a loose, full overcoat with raglan sleeves) or A-line styles. Think twice about belted coats, or cover-ups with lots of darts and stitching details.

Light on top, dark on bottom, or monochromatic outfits create a long line from your waist and de-emphasize the width of the waistline.

lower figured

Knit Jerseys, Tanks, and T-shirts

Consider boatnecks and cap sleeves. Both broaden you on top if you have narrow shoulders. Think twice about bell or flared sleeves as they add extra "weight" to the lower half of your body.

Blouses and Shirts

To flatter, try tailored, lightly fitted shirts; shirts with pocket details, shoulder pad, and other shoulder details such as epaulettes or beadwork; and broad collars. Scoop-neck peasant blouses that are not too voluminous work well with fitted bottoms. Think twice about tops that are too tight or tailored as they may emphasize the smaller proportion of your top.

Jackets and Blazers

Try semifitted styles that end at the hip or flare slightly to cover your bottom. An easy-fitting or "boyfriend" jacket (a straight or slightly A-line style that is long enough to cover your bottom) or a one-button tailored blazer elongates the body. Avoid bolero jackets; waist-length jackets; very boxy, short styles; and double-breasted jackets.

Skirts

Bias-cut, A-line, wrap, fit-and-flare, and straight-cut skirts are becoming. Think twice about wide or contrasting waistbands, back pockets, dramatically pegged or pencil shapes, and full pleats.

Pants

Try flat-front trousers and boot-cut, flared-leg, or straight-leg pants with a slightly lower waist. Pants with a band that hits your true waistline work if the band is narrow. Think twice about peg-legged pants, front pleats, side pockets, a high waist, wide waistbands, palazzo pants, and Capris.

Dresses

To flatter, follow the guidelines for skirts. That means dresses with bias cut and A-line bottoms and fitted tops. Wrap styles are also pretty. Think twice about anything too fitted on the bottom or Empire-waist dresses.

Coats

Try swing, trench, or wrap coats. Avoid balmacaans (loose, full overcoats with raglan sleeves commonly made from twill, wool, or canvas), fitted or highly tailored coats, and double-breasted styles.

Light on top, dark on bottom brings visual weight to your upper torso and balances the bottom.

upper figured

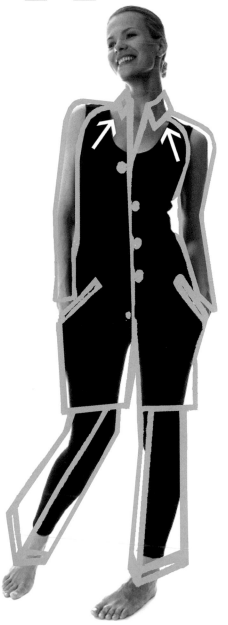

THE SECOND SKIN

Knit Jerseys, Tanks, and T-shirts

To flatter, tunics, flared or swing-cut, bias-cut, long, and fitted tops are soft and pretty. Think twice about cropped Ts, tube tops, strapless tops, or boxy, loose styles.

THE ESSENTIAL TOP

Blouses and Shirts

Stick with straight styles with minimal details. Think twice about shirts with decorative stitching, front-flap pockets, oversized buttons, and excessive embellishment.

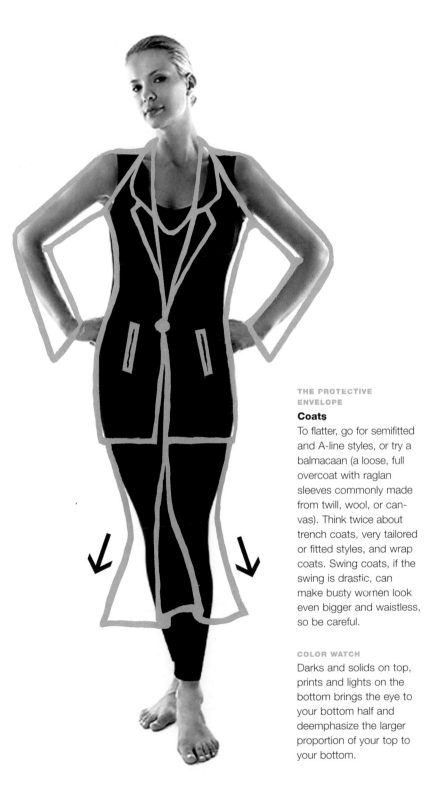

Jackets and Blazers

One-button jackets, long dusters, and swing or bias-cut styles work well. Think twice about fitted, multibuttoned jackets, double-breasted styles, or cropped jackets.

Pants

Try nonpleated but tailored trousers with a smooth front and a narrow waistband or wide-legged, flared, and boot-cut pants because they balance your shape. Think twice about Capris, pleated pants, ankle-length pants, or high waists.

Skirts

Choose A-line, fit-and-flare, and bias-cut styles, and flirty hemlines. Avoid pencil or straight-cut skirts.

Dresses

Semifitted, bias-cut, shirt-dress, coatdress, A-line, lightly swing-cut, and lightly fitted sheath styles all work well. Think twice about Empire waists, cinched waists, and slim-fitting knits.

Coats

To flatter, go for semifitted and A-line styles, or try a balmacaan (a loose, full overcoat with raglan sleeves commonly made from twill, wool, or canvas). Think twice about trench coats, very tailored or fitted styles, and wrap coats. Swing coats, if the swing is drastic, can make busty women look even bigger and waistless, so be careful.

Darks and solids on top, prints and lights on the bottom brings the eye to your bottom half and deemphasize the larger proportion of your top to your bottom.

Save My Neck

Depending on how broad your shoulders are and how long your neck is, different necklines frame your neck, shoulders, bust, and face in unique ways. Here are some simple principles you can use to choose the neckline of your sweaters. As noted in the Second Skin and Essential Top sections of your Shape of Style guide, the neckline makes an impact on the appearance of your neck, chin, face, and even general shape. Remember that details around the neck, including gathering, shirring, ribbons, bows, beading, and piping, automatically draw attention to your neck area and face and away from something else. Food for thought!

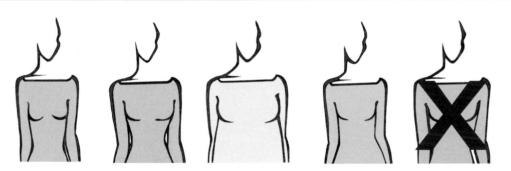

The horizontal line of this neck helps broaden narrow shoulders and balances out a lower-figured woman. Wide boat necks (those with openings that span the width of your shoulders) are great for women with large or small necks and narrow shoulders but are best avoided if you have very broad shoulders or a short neck.

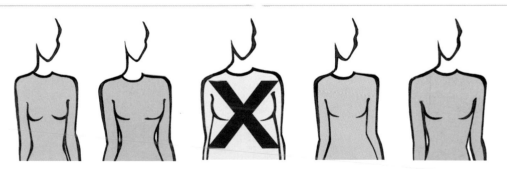

This is the classic T-shirt neckline. The high, rounded style might make a short neck look even shorter. If the neckline hits the bottom of your neck, it can make a cutting, unflattering ring around your neck.

SCOOP OR U

This picture-frame neckline flatters almost everyone. It draws attention to the face without being fussy. This neckline always looks modern.

SQUARE

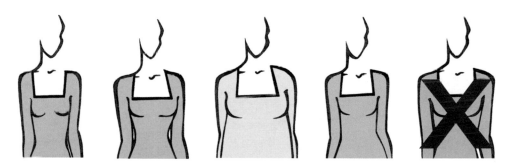

Like a scoop or a U, this style accentuates and frames your face. It's most flattering on narrow-shouldered women. A wide, shallow square makes broad shoulders look wider. It's a nice neckline for balancing lower-figured women.

STRAPLESS

This style come in straight, sweetheart, shirred, and rounded shapes, and others as well. Strapless styles look great on small- or medium-busted women, those with beautiful broader shoulders and long necks.

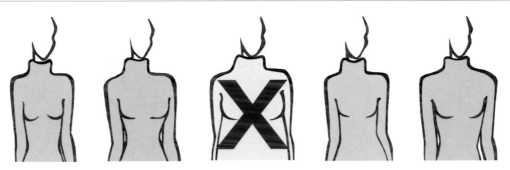

I don't personally find turtlenecks comfortable, but they are flattering to women with long necks, and they can certainly hide flaws (think neck wrinkles). But if you have a very round face, or a short neck, turtle- and cowl necks are best avoided, as they draw attention to that area.

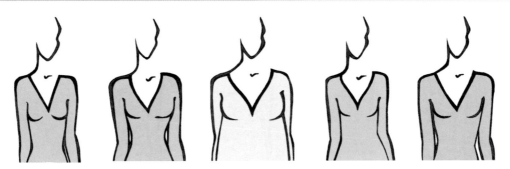

I love V-necks. I think they flatter everyone and create the illusion of a long line and a narrow waist. A wide V-neck flatters those with narrow shoulders; those with broad shoulders benefit from a narrow, deep V. Vs are also very sexy.

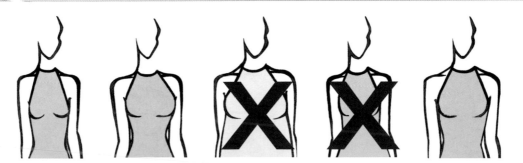

Halter necklines are classic and can be sexy, but they aren't right for everyone. Narrow-shouldered women should avoid this style, as should large-busted women. Halter tops flatter small-busted women and women with broader shoulders. Halter necklines draw the eye down vertically, and for that reason may not be the best choice for lower-figured women.

Have a Fit

The right silhouette in the wrong size doesn't do you any good. Everything you wear has to fit properly for it to fall correctly and drape in a flattering manner. If it's too tight or too big, it's not meant to be; it just won't look right. We ignore fit a lot of times. We'll tell ourselves that it's not too tight just because we love it and it's the only one, or it's on sale, or we just don't want to admit we may take a different size. Who cares?

First, ignore the number on the label. You don't wear clothes inside out, and only the rudest sort would check the size of the clothes you are wearing! There is no standard when it comes to size. You may say that in general you take a size 6 or 10 or 16. But how many times have you grabbed "your" size and had to try one size up or down before you found the size that fit you?

High-end designer clothes, for example, are often cut on the large side—it's a psychological trick to make women think they are smaller than they actually are. Less expensive clothes, on the other hand, often run quite small—so even an extra-large knit top seems so small that it wouldn't fit a five-year-old! Start paying attention to the way the clothes look and feel when you put them on—ignore the number or letter (S, M, L, XL) on the label. Ill-fitting clothes, whether baggy or tight, don't make you appear thinner or smaller—on the contrary, they add pounds. Who wants that?

So how should something fit? If a skirt puckers across the hips or thighs, it's too tight. The same goes for pants. If a blouse buckles at the closings, it's too small. A T can be formfitting, but not so tight that every bulge and bra line is visible. If a dress rides up, take it off. All clothes, including skirts, pants, blouses, jackets, T-shirts, and dresses, should skim the body and close properly without the fabric straining. Pant fronts should lie flat and not hug your tummy. The back should not hug your buns to the point of looking like a body stocking (we've all seen that mistake). Lapels, collars, and waistbands should lie flat and smooth. Full-length

> ## "It is the mind that makes the body."
>
> —Sojourner Truth,
> preacher and civil rights advocate

jacket sleeves should hit your wrist bone—anything longer, and it may look like the jacket is wearing you.

You have more leeway with loosely cut clothing—but something that's cut to be flowing can still be too big, with you ending up swimming in it. So for unstructured pieces it's worth taking the time to try on three different sizes of the same item to find the one you like best. Personally, I think big, loose clothing makes you look bigger. When trying on loose-fitting clothes, give a smaller size a try.

Pant hem length is determined by the heel height of the shoes you wear. Long pants should hit the middle of the top of your foot when worn with flats or midheels (up to 2 inches). Pants worn with high heels (higher than 2 inches) can be a bit longer, so that the hem of the pants covers the back of the shoe completely and allows the heel to show. Capri or midcalf to ankle-length pants are best worn with flats.

Most of all you should feel great when you put on a piece of clothing. You should be able to sit, stand, walk, and move around comfortably, and the clothes should stay in place. They should move with you, not against you! Comfort goes beyond the physical feeling—the outfit itself should make you feel good emotionally as well. We'll talk more about that in chapter 4.

style diary

Skirt the Issue

Whenever you try on a skirt, be sure to play with the waist by rolling it to see how it looks slightly higher on the leg and tighter on your hips—or try on a slightly bigger size to see how it looks when it hangs lower on the hip. One skirt offers a variety of looks when you alter it in this do-it-yourself way. Even one inch can have a tremendous effect because small differences in size can make a big difference. One caveat: a rolled waist must be covered with either a belt or an untucked shirt or jersey that covers the rolled fabric. A dropped waist can show.

Balance and Proportion

Dressing for your shape means more than just choosing the right silhouettes. You have to put them together in a pleasing way. Building a great outfit requires combining elements that relate to one another—in terms of color, texture, scale, and fit—while still creating a bit of tension or irony between them.

Your height, width, and overall size have an impact on the way your clothes look. You know what I'm talking about: you have seen outfits that look "off" not because of any one element but because the whole outfit looks off balance. Everything could be very fashionable, beautifully made, and pretty, but there's something jarring about the way the ensemble presents. This normally occurs when lines of the clothes cut up the body in an unflattering way. For instance, horizontal lines always break up curves and long lines, and unless you are linear figured, this works against you.

A general guideline when putting together a look—and this is especially important when using eclectic elements –is actually quite simple:

- Short top with long bottom
- Long top with short bottom
- Full top with narrow bottom
- Narrow top with full bottom

See the chart on the next page to see what this means.

For example, if you are wearing a long skirt, say midcalf or longer, pair it with a shorter top or jacket. If you are wearing a long skirt, flats work best. Shorter skirts look balanced with high heels. A full peasant blouse with a gathered neck looks chic with narrower pants or a slightly flared skirt but may overwhelm a woman if she wears it with a gathered full skirt. Of course, every guideline has an exception. Sometimes a long tunic that glides smoothly over your frame looks great with palazzo pants of the same fabric.

I recently worked with the beautiful actress Sharon Stone on wardrobe for a film she was making. She put on a very tight, very tiny T in a creamy white. Of course, it fit her beautifully, but I wasn't sure it was right for the character or her figure, which is linear. But then she paired it with a pair of very wide-legged trousers in the same color tone and *wow*,

balance & propo

SHORT TOP WITH LONG BOTTOM

LONG TOP WITH SHORT BOTTOM

rtion guidelines

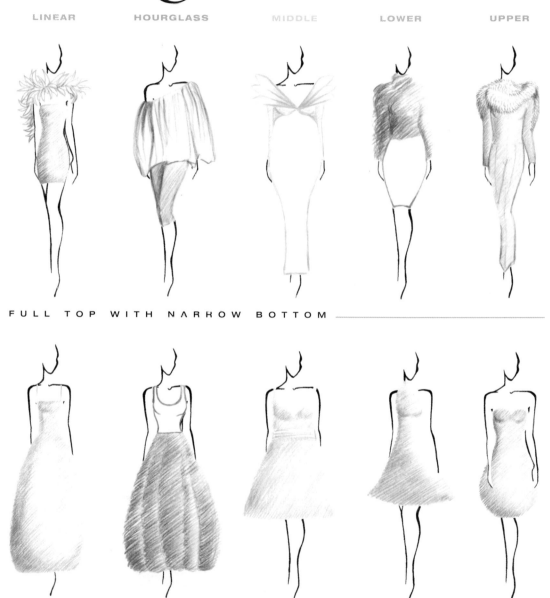

LINEAR   HOURGLASS   MIDDLE   LOWER   UPPER

FULL TOP WITH NARROW BOTTOM

NARROW TOP WITH FULL BOTTOM

it was a striking combination and it created a stunning curve. She knows herself and her body very well. That's an example of great proportion.

You can think of mixing color and texture in a similar way. But in general, too many opposing forces in the same outfit detract from the ensemble. For example, three different tweeds (jacket, pants, and coat) and a busy print blouse add up to overwhelming for those of us taking it all in. A large open print in a skirt might look awkward with a tiny, busy print on top or vice versa. But a pinstripe pant with a print top may look smart, because the two fabrics complement each other directionally and texturally.

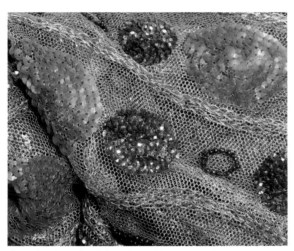
Sequined, embroidered, and beaded tulle

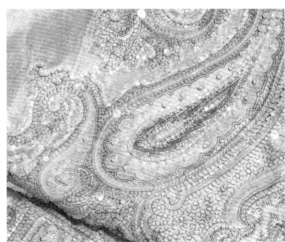
Printed, embellished cotton

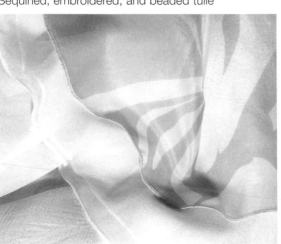
Printed chiffon

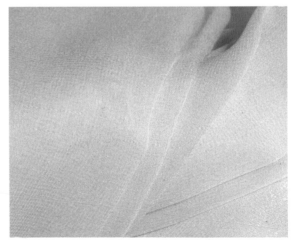
Silk georgette

Recommend Yourself

Honor who you are and what you like. Write a page about yourself in the third person, as if you were writing a recommendation. Describe what you are like as a person, a friend, a spouse, and a lover . . . everything. What's great about you? What do you like to do? How do you enjoy spending time? Write about yourself like a benevolent friend. Describe your best qualities, your personality, your talents, your strengths, interests, and goals. This is a road map to who you are.

_____

_____

_____

_____

_____

_____

_____

_____

_____

_____

_____

_____

_____

_____

_____

_____

style diary

"Fashions fade, but style is eternal."

—Yves Saint-Laurent, clothing designer

CHAPTER 4

make the look your own

DETERMINE AND CULTIVATE YOUR AUTHENTIC STYLE

If you're unhappy with your current
wardrobe and you're not sure what to do
about it, here's your opportunity to change.
There are always subtle shifts going on in
our opinions and the way we live day to
day. A move to a new city or town
certainly makes our life different.
Our clothes must keep up
with our personal evolution.
For example, maybe you want
to develop a more profes-
sional style because you want to
advance in your career. Or you have
reached an age milestone and you want
to shed the suits and pumps of your office
days and indulge in something more whimsical
and fun. Perhaps you're newly active in a charity
or other organization that requires formal socializing,
something you hadn't done too much of in the past.

Now you want to develop a persona around that, with clothes to match. Or you are simply tired of not having a defined style and want to develop one—just for the fun and satisfaction of doing so. The only reason you need to develop personal style is "just because."

It's worth taking the Shape of Style further. Beyond simply finding clothes that suit your figure, you can find those that suit your individuality because clothes change how you look *and* how you feel. Case in point: Recently I spent the day with my friend Tobi (whom you'll meet later in these pages). She is original and stylish and knows herself very well; she's creative, pragmatic, direct, and strong. But on this particular afternoon she was in a foul mood.

Tobi was dressed in a linen jacket with a ruffled collar. I asked her what was wrong, and she just couldn't say, but she did mention in passing that she was not happy with her jacket. And that struck me. I said, "Well, of course. You're not a ruffle!"

She knew *exactly* what I meant—and we both laughed. That ruffle put her in a bad frame of mind. It went against the grain of her personality. We all wear "off" items like that at one time or another. The process of uncovering and unleashing your personal style leads to such errors—think of them as learning experiences, because they are. Tobi was brave enough to try something new. It didn't work, so the jacket was off to the charity shop the next day.

When finding a personal style for the first time or for the first time in several years, it is so important to gravitate to items you love at first sight. Not all of them will be right in the end, but when you are starting, it's more important to unleash yourself. You can edit and refine later. Remember, finding your style is a process that begins with a brainstorm. Not every initial idea makes it into the final product.

So how do you start? First, recognize what really matters: not what I think—but what *you* think and how *you* feel. You might be used to putting a lot of emphasis

your favorite things

Make a list of all the things you truly love—*everything*—and keep it with you, or post it in a place where you can see it every day!

style diary

You most likely have a friend who is close to you in size but maybe not in taste. Even so, I want you to switch closets for a weekend, or even a week. That's right, I want you to wear each other's clothes. Even if you don't love everything, try it all anyway. This is a mind-, and style-, bending exercise. Do you feel like a different person wearing your friend's clothes? Did you find anything you really liked (no swiping—we're just swapping!)? Did you learn anything about your friend's style? What did it tell you about yours? Was wearing your friend's clothes fun, frightening, uncomfortable, or neutral? Think about your feelings—what does the experience tell you about your own style?

on how other people view your clothes (or how you imagine they feel about them). But do you really want to conform to conventional or hackneyed ideas about what you should wear because you're a certain age or live in a certain city or town? Those "shoulds" and "shouldn'ts" can be so confining, and no one cares about them anyway.

We all need to get to a place where we can develop and express ourselves freely without worrying about what others think. Personal style starts with confidence. It's not so much *what* you are wearing; it's *how* you are wearing it. Learn to trust your instincts and follow your heart; your clothes will then embody that certainty and joy. Best of all, self-assured style lets you go from one look to another, because it's always there, supporting you underneath it all. Your style, and your Shape of Style Silhouette, is your foundation—you can always count on them once you've identified them.

As you peel away the layers of fashion ideas you have accumulated over the years, many emotions may come to the surface. Stubborn beliefs about our image and physical appearance hang on tightly; push them aside. The external (what you are wearing) and internal (the feelings your new look evokes) changes that come from finding your style are scary to confront—but ultimately exciting.

I saw an episode of a television fashion show that teaches a valuable lesson about personal style. The show asks people to submit a friend whose style they don't like. The participants are usually pretty resistant to change, and their friends can be really brutal. On this particular episode the woman participant (I'll call her Tess, not her real name) had a very '60s hippie style but not in a self-possessed way. Her outfits were thrown together. Tess had let her appearance go and was obviously unhappy about the situation. She was hiding behind her PhD smarts and somehow ended up believing that style and intelligence were mutually exclusive. Nothing could be further from the truth, of course.

Tess's hair was long and unkempt, and my first impression was, Wow, she's a frumpola with absolutely no sex appeal. In fact, she complained about her lack of dates and general dissatisfaction with the way her life was going. Her friends were fairly stylish, and when they appeared on the show they were very cruel and made a point of trashing her wardrobe figuratively and literally—they threw away a lot of it in a trash can provided by the show. That was very emotional for her.

It was obvious that Tess desperately wanted to change, but she just did not know where to begin. Her clothes had become a habit, a barrier to her sensual feminine side. Anyway, her denim overalls and string ties all went out. They were outdated and not good examples of that particular hippie look. She knew it too, but it was hard for her to admit.

Tess had a lot going for her—she was slim and tall and actually quite pretty under all the clothes and hair. Her friends wanted to gentrify and homogenize her. The outfits they selected were wrong for her personality, and she knew it. Because Tess was not a New York executive, trying to make her look like a generic version of one was not going to work. And even if her friends managed to convince her to dress that way, she would not have stuck with it.

Her two friends and a designer put together three looks for her—including hair and makeup. The host of the show let her choose between the three looks but did not tell her who had put each together. She chose the designer's outfit.

The hippie bohemian idea worked for her, but had just mutated into something awkward and disheveled. The designer wanted to help Tess refine and update her personal style. He wanted to show her the right silhouettes for her shape, which was linear. It made no sense to put her in something frilly and pink or minimalist and black. Straightening her naturally curly hair wasn't going to fly, either—she didn't have the time or the inclination to blow it out straight every day.

The designer had Tess's curls conditioned and trimmed so they looked great in their natural state. Then he selected jeans in a low-rise boot cut to create a nice curve, and a pale peasant-style top with a little embroidery around the neckline and shoulders for glamour and balance. It just met the low waist of the jeans, giving her an easy but elegant look. Brown cowgirl boots and a chocolate suede belt added sex appeal and even more shape. With some dangly earrings and bangle bracelets, she was H-O-T! At the end of the process, she had found a look she liked and felt tuned into. It was influenced by a hippie look, but it was chic and put together. The fit and color of the clothing flattered her figure and coloring. At the end of it all, Tess learned that she didn't have to compromise her identity to look polished, put together, and pretty.

The lesson here is to take what you love, what is inherently part of your personality and lifestyle, and use *that* as a base from which your look can develop. Stay true to your shape, your way of living, and your character, but embrace change when individual pieces or looks no longer work for you.

Along with determining your shape and taking to heart your Shape of Style Silhouette, follow these "rules" to help you develop personal style. I think you'll actually find them freeing—these really aren't the "always" and "never" kind of rules (which I don't believe in when it comes to fashion).

RULE #1: Don't try to conform to anyone else's taste. Your wardrobe should be a reflection of your shape, style, interests, and preferences.

RULE #2: Embrace change. Don't be afraid to try something new. As your life changes, so too can your way of dressing. Try one trendy piece in your Shape of Style Silhouette and see how it makes you feel. Take note of how new-for-you clothes make you feel, and how they feel when you walk, sit, act, and react when you are by yourself and with other people. Turn things upside down: if it is allowed at your office, wear a weekend look to the workplace and see if you like it. What's the reaction? If you don't usually get really dressed up when you go out to dinner, do so next time. Take all opportunities to experiment.

RULE #3: Try it on. Fashion and style are experiential and visual. Simply put, you have to try on the beads and the fringe before you know for sure they are wrong for you because you're truly classic and tailored.

RULE #4: If you put something on and it doesn't feel good, take it off. Even if someone says a piece looks good on you, if you don't feel right in it, don't feel pressured to wear it.

RULE #5: Seek out and wear what you love. You can't go wrong if you live life like this. So many of us dress for other people in order to represent an image of how they think we should look or match a notion about how we need to dress because we are a certain age. And it doesn't make us happy. Ask yourself, Do you *like* your style and your clothes, or do you simply feel comfortable in them? Has your wardrobe become a habit? This rule doesn't conflict with the notion that you have to get out of your comfort zone and try new things; so many women end up in a fashion place they don't like because they feel they must dress a certain way to please others. Indulge your fantasies and desires; finding clothes and accessories that work for your shape and that you honestly like results in change.

style guide

Start the Process:
Discover What You Love

A woman came to me not long ago to apply for a job as my personal assistant. As the interview went along it was evident from her demeanor that this woman had mixed feelings about doing this sort of work. She was at a crossroads in her life and didn't quite know what direction to take. She obviously had a lot of flair and style, so I asked her, "Why are you so confused—what do you love?" It turned out it was jewelry design. She showed me her designs, and I saw that she was very artistic. So instead of hiring her (she agreed that it wasn't the best job for her) I said I would send her to a couple of people who could help her develop her talent into a career.

I tell this story because I think the same goes for personal style. Showing off your style and expressing yourself through your choices is part and parcel of doing what you love in life. Like the woman in the story, you might be reaching for a job or a relationship that you know in your heart isn't right—just as you reach for the ratty old T-shirt for the hundredth time or the navy suit in the wrong cut that ultimately bores you to death. Your job, the hobbies you enjoy, how you live your life, how you dress—it's all part of the same package.

> ## "Good taste is the worst vice ever invented."
>
> **—Dame Edith Sitwell,**
> poet, critic, and biographer

It's easy for me to say, "Develop personal style for yourself," but I do think all of us long to have people say, "You look pretty; you look gorgeous." It would be nice if someone was there to help you get dressed, but most of you do it alone. So by all means, enlist the help of a trusted friend as you take the journey toward defining your own authentic look.

Develop inner confidence and trust in your eye, and the appreciative response that you crave will come calling. In the meantime, applaud yourself.

Know thyself is the ultimate mantra for anything in life. To help you create a plan for getting dressed, we're going to take a personal inventory. This step, like knowing your shape, leads to becoming more self-owned. Have your blue-sky moment—let yourself dream and have fun. It's not so much about knowing that you like roses more than exotic flowers that tells you what to wear. Your likes and dislikes in terms of art, culture, books, et cetera do not necessarily determine your personal style. But they can help inform it by providing inspiration.

My friend Merle, who was photographed for this book, loves the 1920s, especially the British literary figures known as the Bloomsbury Group. Merle doesn't slavishly re-create a '20s flapper look, but much of what she wears has a vintage feel, especially her accessories. The colors used in the design of that period often work their way into her outfits—even those that are very up-to-the-minute. The colors are her secret way of celebrating another age. Merle is also thoroughly modern, has homes on both the East and West coasts, and embraces contemporary and eclectic design. Like fashion itself, she and all of us are full of contradictions. Exploit them!

In addition to outside influences, your personality is also defined by your spirit and nature. Are you good-natured, strong-willed, friendly, evasive, adventurous, curious, regimented, shy, or outgoing? Do you like being the center of attention or the supporter in the background? The answers don't create a rule book. Think about it. You're shy, but you love the Rolling Stones—or acid rock. *Shy* may not mean you need to listen to soft music or wear pastel colors. Personal style comes down to how you want to *feel,* and part of that is rooted in your lifestyle and your preferences.

At this point you might be saying, "Okay, Randolph, I'm this and that; now tell me what I should wear." But that's not it. There's no predetermined formula. You have to tell *yourself* what to wear! By recognizing your personal traits, you just become aware of which aspects you want to play up and which you want to moderate. That's the purpose of a personality inventory. Once you are clear on what you like, you can make natural choices without overanalyzing or overdoing a look.

Know yourself and you will never be a fashion victim. When Seventh Avenue tells a woman that minimalism is in and she goes along with it 100 percent, *that's* a fashion victim. Instead, find yourself—in every way! Find your perfect career, joy, happiness, and the ability to express who you are. Be confident in your choices. If you want to wear a limited range of color, do it. If you're partial to vintage, wear vintage.

Make a list of all the things you truly love—everything. For instance, I like reading more than I like movies; I like trucks better than sports cars; I like country music more than pop. The list becomes a guide to self-expression and keeps you from falling into the trap of looking like a page in a fashion magazine. When you are conscious of the things in life you love, your preferences in clothes naturally become clearer. If you have a passion for opera, start collecting beautiful evening dresses to wear at live performances. If you're a doctor who digs country-and-western music, dress up that white lab coat with cowboy boots (that's what my thoroughly urban New York City dermatologist does).

Inject a sense of fun into the process. You may secretly want to wear certain clothes. Make a mental note of them when you go to a store and try them on. You always end up with interesting surprises when you do that. How do you feel when you are wearing a washed vintage western shirt with jeans versus a black skirt and a crisp white shirt? If you aren't a dress person, or don't think you are, how do you feel when you wear a dress? Do you walk differently? Do people react to you differently? Do you like it? Half the time women think a type of clothing isn't for them, based on an item they tried in the past that was in the wrong silhouette for their shape. All of a sudden, once you know your Shape of Style, the ethnic prints you have always adored (and studied intently on a trip to Africa or Morocco) look smashing on you!

Now that you have the Shape of Style information, spread your wings and enjoy the freedom it gives you. Maybe something you were afraid of ends up looking better than expected. Or your fears are validated when you realize that the shirt or the pants don't look so good after all. Even when someone says, "That looks good on you," if you don't think so—in fact, you

> "Style is a simple way of saying complicated things."
>
> —Jean Cocteau, artist

know it doesn't—go with your instinct. It's like when someone says, "The soup tastes good." If it doesn't taste good to you, *it doesn't taste good*. Period. There's really no debate, is there? I see girls trying things on and their clenched teeth and squinty eyes tell me what I need to know. I say, "Take it off!"

I can hold up two tops and you can tell me which one you like better in seconds. Try it yourself in a store with a friend. Go with your first inclination and see what happens. Have her pick like items (pants, tops, scarves, etc.) two by two. Choose between what she holds up in less than five seconds. Review your choices—I bet they not only form a style guide, but that you also won't change your mind about your choices if you go back to them half an hour later. It all starts with your gut.

That means embracing a little risk. A while ago I worked with the gorgeous actress Angelina Jolie. She wanted to wear something white and very Grace Kelly to an awards show. I wanted her to consider something different, a simple bathing suit–style dress completely encrusted with aged crystals. She was skeptical, but I urged her to try it. "You can always take it off," I said. (Remember that the next time you go into the dressing room—if you can put it on, you can remove it!) Initially, Angelina didn't think she could wear such a high-glamour dress, but the idea intrigued her. When she put it on, it was *wow*, all the way around. I could tell by the look in her eyes that she was excited and titillated by this dress. And it looked stunning. She ended up wearing it and tossing aside the original idea. She was willing to take a risk because she knows herself well.

If you are fascinated and excited by the thought of wearing something different, try it. Don't focus too much on, "What are people going to think of it?" If you are unsure about something but attracted to it, it doesn't mean it's not good for you. It means you should try it and walk around in it for a day and see how you feel. If it lifts your mood, it's right. Go with it.

> "Feel free to play with trends—but always be faithful to your personality and lifestyle."
>
> —Randolph Duke

Learning to Look:
Interpret Fashion Images for Yourself

A walk through a department store or a flip through the pages of a fashion magazine can make choosing clothes an overwhelming exercise. There are too many choices—and who has time to sort through all of them?

Instead of getting discouraged by the disparate images and clothes competing for your attention, view a trip to the store or a flip through *Vogue* as an opportunity to test your taste. What do you see that you like? What do you see that you *don't* like? The great thing about understanding your body type and personal style is that you can disregard or dismiss items quickly and home in on those that meet your personal specifications.

You'll also be more willing to take chances on things you would not ordinarily have looked at or tried on in the past. Because you have built up your confidence and know what shapes work and don't work, taking a chance or breaking the rules doesn't seem as terrifying.

In the store, slow down; take one item at a time and really see its shape. Doing so helps you think visually without becoming flooded with too many competing ideas. Fashion is so diverse, and only the most tyrannical fashion designer would expect you to dress head to toe in his or her clothes. There is always something new in the styles you like. For example, you'll almost always find new twists on classic silhouettes such as a tweed blazer or tailored pants—the lapels on the blazer might be cut wider or narrower; the jacket might be more nipped in at the waist; the pants might have cuffs or not, or a 1-inch slit on the sides; or the colors might be updated.

If you are into the preppy look, for example, you'll always be able to choose between new and interesting items in denim or prints or even plaids, and you can build a wardrobe by adding fresh pieces or replacing others that have lost their allure for you or have become dated. Technology gives us more options every year, too—there are so many absolutely amazing synthetic fabrics these days and every high-end designer is using them. Don't be put off by new materials—instead, see what they do for you.

To keep a magazine page-through from getting confusing, slow down. Fashion magazines should not be used as the gospel for how to dress that season or that month. They are not dictates on what you must buy. In fact, sometimes photos in magazines or ensembles at runway shows are put together to make a very exaggerated point about a trend, not a specific look.

If you see a runway image that shows a model with several different colors of iridescent eye shadow applied up to her eyebrows, her hair "glued" into a gravity-defying do, and her clothes a cacophony of textures, prints, and colors, know that the designer most likely did not mean for that ensemble to be taken literally. The same is true when you see artistic or high-concept images in fashion magazines. You can use these artistic images to discern the shapes, textures, and colors the designer is interested in using that season, or the influences on his or her work: bohemian, India, 1930s art deco, whatever. If those elements appeal to you, some version of the look is available in stores.

Stay current with what high-end designers are doing. When you find a picture of a designer outfit that is clearly meant to show off the clothes in a more realistic, wearable manner, mine the image for clues as to what colors and textures will be offered in the stores that season. The best way to do this is to tear the page out of the magazine so you can focus on it and break it down, away from the cacophony of other images in the magazine. Examine each part of the outfit individually—cut, color, shape, length, fabric. What are the major components of the outfit? Sometimes a single special piece makes it a "look." It could be the pants or the skirt or the top. Which pieces are similar to what you already have, and what aspect of the look can you add to your existing wardrobe? What element(s) do you need to add to complete your interpretation? You may find the only additions necessary are a belt and a piece of jewelry. If you find

pop goes the style

One of my favorite tricks to add additional flair is what I call "Pop the collar and push the sleeves." Doing so creates instant style and flair—every time. I went to dinner with my friend Sandy not that long ago and she had on a trench coat that I designed when I was at Halston. "Do you recognize this?" she asked. It took me a minute, because I wasn't expecting to see her wearing it. I found myself naturally pulling the collar straight up so it framed her neck and pushing up the sleeves so that the narrow wrist hole held all the fabric in place. It looked terrific and brand-new.

an outfit you really love, I don't think it is a bad idea to try to interpret it closely—outfits in magazines are assembled by fashion editors and stylists who know how to put elements together into one cohesive outfit. You can learn a tremendous amount from looking at what they do.

Discover Your Ways of Dressing

There are a few very broad, or umbrella, categories of dressing that have been popular for some time and—a prediction—will continue to be in the future. I don't advocate a "one of these is you" philosophy. You may fit into one of the categories, or feel you are a combination of two or more. However, these major styles of dress will inspire outfit ideas and aid you in developing your personal style. Use the Shape of Style guidelines in chapter 3 to pinpoint the most flattering silhouettes within each way of dressing. I've given you a few examples of such outfits in each section below as a springboard for your own search.

CLASSICISM has a particular fashion vocabulary to choose from, which is fairly specific. It's tailored and fitted and understated, whether a preppy suburban woman or an urban woman expresses it. It can also be "safe" and a bit boring if you don't allow yourself the pleasure of shaking it up with some personal touches that veer away from the classic and create an appealing tension. For example, pairing a classic navy blazer skirt suit with a sleek athletic tank or a silky camisole spices up an otherwise staid outfit.

If you are a classic woman, it's not a bad idea to upset the apple cart once in a while. Try distinctive interpretations of classics and see what you think. Maybe you can wear the same classic components—blazer, pants, and shirt—in a cacophony of bright colors or a sophisticated and monochromatic blend of modern muted tones. The blue blazer, white shirt, and camel pants can be brightened up with a classic but colorful

73

twill scarf or a multitude of chain belts. Or filling the lapel of the blazer with your collection of vintage bumblebee pins sets the office buzzing (remember, odd numbers work best—three, five, or dare you . . . seven?).

Perhaps the pants are in a modern boot cut and the jacket is a classic and flattering one-button style while the shirt reflects the latest trend in color or cut. Or maybe you take the ordinary mother-of-pearl buttons off your white shirt and sew on some vintage rhinestone beauties, African beads, or other pretty, modern, or quirky fasteners. Or you wear the classic outfit—the black suit and white shirt—and top off the whole thing with a thick choker of Indian beads or an elaborate charm bracelet on your wrist. Put together timeless gabardine trousers and a cashmere twinset, but instead of pumps or loafers, throw on a pair of ornate cowboy boots. These sorts of choices turn classical slightly on its head.

URBAN CHIC is a modern, minimal, sophisticated, streamlined version of the classic style. A black cashmere turtleneck, black pants, and contemporary clean-lined silver jewelry worn with designer heels is a good example of classic urban chic. Wearing a Pucci print dress, simple silver or gold hoop earrings, and black high heels is another way to interpret urban chic. The print may not be minimal in and of itself, but the simple lines of the dress and the basic accessories keep it within the minimal vernacular. And Pucci is considered a classic.

Linear and hourglass women have the easiest time finding tailored classic and urban chic clothes that fit their shapes. For example, they can wear natty double-breasted blazers, a style other figure types should avoid. In fact, many of the recommended silhouettes for hourglass and linear women fall into the classic category. That does not mean other Shapes of Style can't wear classic; they can.

Middle-figured women might choose straight-cut one-button blazers and jackets with details, such as a gold insignia button in front and three or four on the bottom of the sleeve, that give this less traditional cut a classic

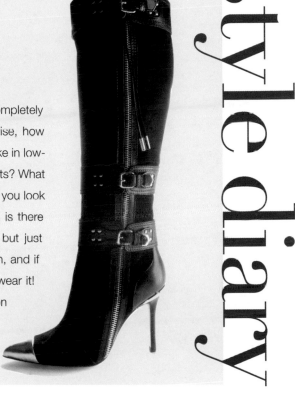

I Wouldn't Be Caught Dead in That . . . or Would I?

The next time you're shopping, select five completely implausible items and try them on. Otherwise, how are you ever going to know what you look like in low-rise jeans, a cropped sweater, or stiletto boots? What do you think? Is there a smile forming when you look at yourself? Now that you've come this far, is there something you've always wanted to wear but just didn't have the nerve to try? Find it, try it on, and if it's not outrageously expensive, buy it and wear it! Develop a willingness to go out on a fashion limb. Remember, they're only clothes.

look. Gray or taupe flat-front straight-cut pants with a narrow waistband teamed with a V-neck white knit top are good alternatives to high-waist trousers and a button-down blouse (silhouettes linear and hourglass women would wear). The lower-figured woman looks good in a blazer or a jacket with a fuller cut on the bottom, paired with a boot-cut pant with a low-rise waist. The top can be a jersey or a button-down shirt. Upper-figured women create a classic look with a straight duster-style jacket in a classic color and team it with a cashmere or silk jersey turtleneck or scoop-neck T and man-tailored pants with cuffs.

BOHEMIAN ETHNIC dressing is often a soft look that depends on ethnic and handmade clothing in fluid fabrics. These pieces often have handcrafted touches such as embroidery, unique closures, or block-printed fabric patterns. (In block printing, a block of wood is carved with a design, dipped in fabric paint or fiber dye, and stamped onto the material.) The "rich hippie" look is also part of this style vernacular. Ethnic jewelry from indigenous cultures is an important component of this style; such one-of-a-kind items are sometimes found at craft fairs, boutiques, and galleries.

In my experience, women who are drawn to the bohemian ethnic style do not limit themselves to clothing inspired or made by just one culture. Instead, they take the best of a variety of ethnic designs—Indian, Native American, African, Eastern European, et cetera—and blend them. They also add contemporary handmade American pieces, sometimes

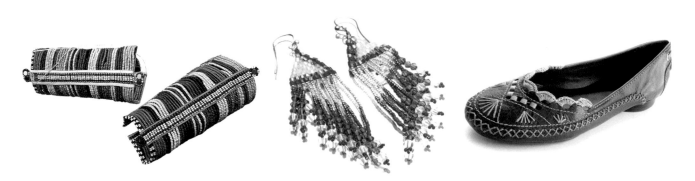

known as wearable art. The bohemian ethnic dresser might pick up a patchwork skirt or a quilted and hand-painted jacket at a craft fair. Or she might mix a string of Venetian glass beads with modern silver or gold pieces by a jewelry artist bought at a local gallery.

When you wear ethnic clothes, you convey a well-traveled, artistic aura. In fact, if you love ethnic clothes, the best place to find them is when you're on a trip to another country. And for a touch of irony, ethnic items can be added, as with classic looks (see above). A great carved bracelet from Africa or an Asian silk jacket is a marvelous conversation starter, too. So don't discount that idea when you are getting dressed for a party.

Many ethnic and craft-show clothes are straight, loose, and made from flowing fabrics, which are all perfect choices for a middle-figured woman. But not all ethnic or culturally inspired clothing is unconstructed

signature style

Many fashionable women include a signature element in their style. A signature is usually one element that is always incorporated into your look or outfit and is recognizably "you." It transcends fashion. It can be a little bob haircut, à la Anna Wintour, that you maintain despite trends in hairstyle. Or it can be a certain pair of sunglasses (think Jackie O), a scent, a favorite pin, or even "signature" pink pants (you may own *dozens*!). Or maybe you always wear an Hermès or other special scarf with your outfit— maybe you always use one as a belt for your jeans. Or you never leave the house without your diamond studs (real or faux) in your ears. You get the idea.

Your signature can also make a statement. A while ago I had dinner with a woman I was meeting for the first time. She was dressed in purple from head to toe. At first I thought, Hmmm, I'm not sure. . . . But over the course of the evening I saw that she was *so* strong and *so* smart. Purple was her signature color, even though her style was basically classic. When I asked her about it, she said, "I love purple, and no one will make me not wear purple." Brava! By the end of the evening, I loved the way she looked. She is a completely self-realized woman. It's not a look for everyone, and I am not advocating it for you. But *she* loved it and conveyed that very clearly. Attitude and confidence are everything!

A signature is a lot of fun, but it's not an essential component of personal style. If you like the idea of having a signature piece, go for it. If not, you can certainly have a style that is definitively yours without one.

in style, so if you are drawn to the ethnic style, you can find looks that are right for your shape. For example, jeans and denim skirts are a great foil for ethnic tops and accessories. Pair your Shape of Style–chosen jeans with an embroidered ethnic blouse or a beaded T. An upper-figured woman looks great in tight jeans, a T-shirt, and a belt with a Native American silver-and-turquoise buckle. Or she can wear a full, gathered Moroccan skirt with a fitted T and beaded slippers.

The lower-figured woman can wear her jeans with an untucked embroidered peasant blouse. Or she can wear a bias-cut Indian-print skirt, topped with a simple V-neck T with lots of amber or coral beads wrapped around her neck. The hourglass woman can wear a fitted version of ethnic pieces or pair a fitted top with a flowing bottom to balance the look. For example, an Austrian forest-green fitted boiled-wool jacket would spark interest paired with wide-legged pants in African kente cloth (a handwoven fabric often combining rich yellows, greens, oranges, and browns) and simple boots. The linear woman can wear her jeans with elaborate quilted wrap jackets, or put together a safari jacket tied at the waist with a belt of the same fabric, an Eastern European peasant skirt, and cowboy boots.

VINTAGE/RETRO dressing can be contrived or elegant. Whether it's '60s mod or romantic Victorian, it's not an easy look to pull off, especially when done head to toe. You have to be careful with vintage clothing. I feel strongly that it's usually best (not to mention more modern looking) to use contemporary elements as a backdrop for vintage garments—that is, to temper vintage with new. Otherwise you end up looking like you are wearing old clothes, or a costume. In general, a vintage look can be achieved successfully via single pieces (a great 1930s coat or blazer, a 1950s retro circle skirt, or a 1970s pop art print shirt) or accessories. Period pieces are powerful, and often one or two is all you need to make an outfit.

Condition is key when buying vintage clothing. Check that any item you are considering is in good shape. Holes, frays, and stains are hard, if not impossible, to fix. Fit and cut are factors, too. Don't buy anything until you try it on. Manufacturers are constantly changing the way they cut clothes, and even a size 10 skirt made as late as the 1980s may not be cut the same way that a similar garment would be today.

Age plays a factor in wearing vintage, too. A woman wearing clothes from the '50s or '60s of her youth could end up looking like she just has not bought any new clothes in forty years! That woman might be better off with a timeless, clean-lined dress and a vintage accessory, such as archetypal Miriam Haskell earrings, to convey a vintage style.

If you've got the antique and collectible clothes bug, take my advice and begin with the simple backdrop of your Shape of Style basic top and bottom, then start adding vintage extras. The middle-figured woman might add shoes, a handbag, and earrings from the 1960s to her basic top and bottom. The linear woman might throw an elaborately embroidered 1930s Spanish piano shawl over her pants and top (they make great wraps). The lower-figured woman could add a bit of old-fashioned charm to her basic canvas with long strands of 1920s flapper-style pearls and a cloche hat from the same period. The upper-figured woman might find a bias-cut all-over print skirt from the 1940s that would look great with a modern, straight-cut T skimming over the waistline. The hourglass woman can find a 1950s Dior-inspired dress with a fitted bodice and full skirt—but team it with modern stilettos and a contemporary, structured handbag.

ECLECTIC STYLE is an artistic melding of disparate styles (classic, bohemian ethnic, retro) and contrasting textures (hard and soft; masculine and feminine, such as denim and silk, leather and satin, tweed and chiffon) into one triumphant look. More and more people fall into this category of dressing or identify with it. I think it's because it offers so many options and ways to express intentions, desires, and fantasies. It allows a woman to indulge her love of clothes and fashion.

Eclecticism is challenging to pull off successfully. For one thing, eclectic dressing demands that you not play it safe. You're always on the edge of disaster—combining one too many of the latest trends in a single look can turn a fashion vixen into a fashion victim. It's a thrill ride.

Dressing this way requires you to spend time combining different style elements to find just the right ones. If you think you might want to try your hand at developing an eclectic look, do it! It's going to be a long time before we move away from eclecticism and irony in dress. Yes, maybe the fashion editors say last year was all about embroidery and beading and embellishment and this year it's about minimalism and simplicity, but those "trends" are created each year to sell a whole new line of fashion. And very few women want or need to be dictated to. I say as long as your silhouettes are right for your shape, it is anything goes, all the time. In other words, take all the ways of dressing described in this chapter and mix them up!

STATEMENT DRESSING is a visual way of making a public announcement, loud and clear. It is the most rarified style, because it's the most constraining by its very nature. I once met a woman in New York's Hamptons beach community while visiting my favorite thrift store, ARF (all the proceeds go to help animals). I noticed a couple who looked out of place to me in this upscale area. They were a motorcycle couple dressed 1960s style. The woman had very black hair and she was wearing too much eyeliner, bright blue eye shadow, and extremely tight clothes. Her husband had an Elvis pompadour. They certainly stood out!

The woman came up to me and said, "You're that guy on TV! You're that man who helps women!" Her well-intentioned fumbling got us into a lively conversation. This couple intrigued me. At the time I was developing a TV show that was to be a style boot camp for women. Participants would go away for a month or so and discover their personal style. To qualify, you had to be unhappy about your look.

I described the premise of the show to this woman and asked if she would be interested in going to L.A. to film the pilot. Without hesitation she replied, "No, I love the way I look."

Her response made me pause, and then I said, "Congratulations. You're fabulous." She was quite premeditated about the way she dressed. She knew who she was and announced it with her clothes. Her husband did, too—in fact, their fashion declaration was even clearer as a couple. This woman wasn't about to join a fashion regime—her look was derived from a very inward place. *That's* statement dressing.

Another example of statement dressing is the woman who always wears black, even in the heat of summer. Or one who makes a political or social statement by always dressing in fatigues and T-shirts and sneakers and who chooses not to shave her legs. Statement dressing is full of deliberate drama. It's less about fulfilling specific intentions (which we'll learn about in the next chapter) and more about making a consistent point. For example, I doubt the Elvis lady would dress any differently at a black-tie ball (maybe her jacket would have a few less nail-head studs) or at her job. Statement clothes are the means to the message that often goes beyond what's worn. It's costume in the most literal sense.

You can make your statement and still benefit from the Shape of Style Silhouette guidelines. The Elvis woman was an hourglass, so her tight, fitted clothes were not inappropriate for her shape. If she was linear, her Elvis look might have needed more embellishment at the waist and shoulders to create a curve. If she were upper figured, boot-cut jeans and a longer, hip-length leather jacket would suit her, and still get the message across. A lower-figured Elvis-lover might wear a cropped leather jacket with epaulettes. Let's just say that if you have something to say with your clothes, you can find a silhouette that allows the statement to be figure flattering.

Perhaps a lightbulb went off over your head when you read one or more of the descriptions above because you've always had a certain look in mind but didn't quite know how to define it. Or maybe this section will inspire you and help you formulate or define your own look and style. Maybe you'll come up with a new term for your way of dressing and create a brand-new fashion language! How about Suburban Retro or Urban Southern or European Modern? What do they mean to you? Do these names stir up any ideas? See what you can come up with—it's part of the fun of getting dressed.

Pulling It Together

No matter what your personal style, there are fundamentals to building a look and a wardrobe that have to do with form and function. Here are the basic wardrobe building blocks.

Pull Focus

An outfit, like a room, looks best when it has a focal point. Too many attention-getters in one look confuses the eye and translates as a jumble of ideas. The essence of personal style is having a point of view. So decide on the central element—all other elements and accessories should relate back to that central element, which, by the way, can be a jacket, a string of pearls, a pair of shoes, or even a coat. The focal point is usually your personality piece. It's your bold stroke! Read more about the personality piece in chapter 9.

Inspirations and Authentic Style

- Choose a couple of fashion magazines you like and read them for a few months each season to get an idea of what's out there. Perusing shopping magazines such as *Lucky* is a good way of keeping up with trends and seeing options in a variety of price ranges.
- Go to the store and try on lots of clothes—try things you love as well as things you don't like or never thought about wearing before and see what happens.
- Look to women you admire (actresses or that stylish coworker) and ask yourself why. Break down their choices into components.
- Develop your eye by taking in the world around you!

Catch Some Color

Color is an emotional, personal choice. It is as simple as saying, "I like orange; I don't care for pink." If you feel good wearing blue, by all means we should be putting you in blue. Generally, you want to use colors that flatter your complexion near your face. Experiment with the many new color tones on the market to find shades that flatter you. In other words, all blues are not created equal. Blue is pretty, but try holding Kelly green up to your face and you may see that it does a lot more for your complexion, eyes, and hair. Be willing to try colors you've never worn!

Well-chosen colors always get a positive reaction. When people spontaneously say, "You look radiant" or "You really look great," most of the time it's attributed to the color you're wearing and how it reflects light on your face.

An eclectic look can be unified through color. Colors that either blend or complement one another help link different styles and periods. For example, a red Indian peasant blouse with black-and-silver embroidery can be paired with 1940s-style black man-tailored trousers with a little white or gray pinstripe. You can add either modern wedge shoes in black or red, or little gold flats, and modern silver jewelry and a vintage metal handbag. Finish it off with a black knit wrap. Or think about using color accents (jewelry, bag, shoes, etc.) with neutral pieces to connect different elements.

Black, white, and gray are compatible with every color, and they can also act as connectors between colors. They can brighten a color or bring a patterned piece under control. If you want to balance an intensely colored top, pair it with a gray or a muted version of the bright tone. Deep, vivid colors are tougher to combine with brights and pastels, but browns and other dark colors can enrich their intensity and depth, as can natural neutral colors. Pale, muted colors and pastels complement deep, dark grayish and neutral tones. Vivid colors or brights look great with black and white. And black can complement a muted pattern.

Create Some Tension

Eclectic style is all about contrast—but even if you are putting together a more traditional outfit, keep in mind the juxtaposition of pieces. There should always be some tension in the outfit—it creates movement and life. A rough tweed hacking jacket looks more interesting when paired with a satiny blouse and floaty skirt than it would with the more conventional ribbed turtleneck and jeans. A red "power suit" reaches a whole new level if worn with a jersey top in a Pucciesque pop art print or a little leopard-print T rather than with a white cotton shirt or a navy silk blouse. Beaded high-heeled mules with jeans and a white T and chandelier earrings can make a dinner date hotter than a "little black dress." Do you see where I'm going?

Balance the Act

Mixing too many textures and prints can create havoc on your body and start a panic in the streets. Try for harmony in your outfit. If it's all black, crisp, smooth, and minimal on the bottom and all pastel, tweedy, woolly, thick, and bejeweled on top, the outfit looks off. Better to bring one element to the top or bottom of an outfit. So, for example, balance the black pants and tweed jacket with a pair of embellished—beaded or patterned—highly decorated shoes. It's that offbeat shoe that balances a more conservative pairing.

Edit It

What you leave in the closet or the drawer is just as important as what you are wearing—once you're dressed, take a long look at yourself in a full-length mirror and assess the ensemble one last time. If you think something looks "off" or extraneous, it probably is—remove it.

Have a Sense of Whimsy

Remember not to overthink your outfit. Don't lose your sense of humor or your spontaneity. Your "second thoughts" are often less successful than your

style diary

Storyboard

Creating an inspiration board for your own life and style is a great way to pull together all of your preferences. And it's a nice object to hang in your dressing area. Interior designers create inspiration boards for their clients. I am sure you have seen these and you may have even created one before you redecorated a room. Well, you can do the same thing for your personal style.

First, collect fabric swatches in textures and colors you love, paint chips that express your moods, photographs of yourself that you love from different periods in your life, and favorite fashion images from magazines. Cut them out and mount them on a piece of poster board. Mount swatches on small pieces of foam board that you can also paste on the poster board in order to create different levels. Have fun putting it together (think of it as a scrapbooking project—only for your wardrobe!).

initial ideas. Trust your gut, do something fun, and don't take it too seriously!

I urge you to take the time to be unique and different in your choices. Don't do something just because everyone is doing it. Eventually, you'll be able to put together an outfit in seconds. For certain events—a hot first date or an important job interview, for example—it will take more time to assess what it is you want your outfit to do. It's less about "Is it right?" and more about "Does it serve my purpose?" That's intention dressing, which is covered in the next three chapters.

NAME: Merle Ginsberg

OCCUPATION: entertainment and fashion journalist

SHAPE: hourglass

STYLE: Literary Romantic

INTENTION: "To be singular but also appropriate to the occasion and to myself."

INSPIRATION: "Bloomsbury and the 1920s. Coco Chanel is always in the back of my mind.

PHILOSOPHY: "If you are going to wear a uniform, it should be chiffon! You could drink champagne in any of my clothes!"

MOTTO: "If all else fails, go to Barneys!"

merle Ginsberg is tall, sexy, and smart. Her passion for literature and an interest in what's going on in the worlds of fashion and design inform her taste. "I always have a little 1920s thing going on," she says. "So many people are trying to look like anyone but themselves, probably because society does not reward individuality."

Her circa 2000 Dolce & Gabbana leopard-print chiffon dress reveals just the right amount of skin. "It's my idea of a classic dress," she says. Under a coat it's perfect for a fall or winter cocktail party, and on its own it's a beautiful look for warm evenings on the town. It is slightly fitted and flatters Merle's long curves. Jan Stanton's company, Heartfelt, made the velvet hat.

wild card

NAME: Shawn King

OCCUPATION: mom/wife/recording artist

SHAPE: upper figured

STYLE: Natural Woman/Chameleon

INTENTION: "I want to be appropriate for all the events and roles in my life. I wear a lot of hats, as a mother and wife, a performer, and chairperson of the Larry King Cardiac Foundation."

INSPIRATION: "My life and my children. I don't want to be so trendy that twenty-five years from now I have a 'What was I thinking?' moment when I look at pictures of myself."

PHILOSOPHY: "Dress for the occasion, but aim for elegance and fun— save extremism for the special moments."

Shawn King is one of the nicest people you'll ever meet. She's warm, down to earth, and devoted to her family, which includes two sons and a high-profile husband, CNN powerhouse Larry King. That means Shawn is on the go from morning to night—she dresses up *a lot.*

Shawn loves this Audrey Hepburn–ish satin-and-chiffon dress with butterflies. "This is a really special dress. I would not wear it to someone else's function. You have to be aware that it's their day," she says graciously. The matching wrap is embellished with black, gray, and white butterflies.

TAMARA This outfit is a perfect example of style meets comfort. The strapless silk top tied with a sash to create an Empire bodice and petal like hem floats in watery shades of green. It's the perfect complement to a linear figure because it creates lots of movement and curves. Under the top, Tamara is wearing brown canvas shorts! "I would wear this outfit to a party or a public event because it is such a showpiece," Tamara says.

The shoes are by Jimmy Choo (of course!). The chandelier earrings are from India. "I love mixing prints and colors with Indian jewelry," she says. A Japanese straightening system keeps her long hair groomed. "I can just get up and go. I don't have time for blowouts."

TOBI Tobi's grandmother inspired this outfit. "The Native American jewelry was hers," she explains. "I started with these pieces and built the outfit from there."

The pashmina is a practical accessory that adds a splash of color. The cotton skirt is long, tiered, and slightly gathered. Mexican-inspired embroidery embellishes the top, which just covers the waistline of the skirt and floats over Tobi's waist in a very flattering way. The low-slung western-style belt peeks out slightly, adding a little playful mystery. The silk flower pinned to her chic, pulled-back hair adds even more femininity to this pretty ensemble.

CONSTANCE This outfit would certainly stop traffic— even in Times Square! "Grace Jones is my inspiration for this nightclub, evening-out-on-the-town look because she is over the top and a recurring fashion icon," says Constance. The gold lamé leather trench was borrowed from a friend.

Notice how the belt is tied to cinch the waist. The Masai tribe made the incredible cuffs and neckpiece.

Makeup this dramatic should be applied by an expert. "This is out of bounds. We studied Grace Jones's look and then superimposed it on my face," says Constance of makeup pro Tobi Britton's work.

SANDY Sandy discovered this incredible 1920s kimono at a Paris flea market. "When I put this on I feel glamorous and totally decadent. I actually wore this to the Oscars," says Sandy. The kimono's silhouette would flatter most every shape, and it looks particularly regal on Sandy's tall frame.

The vintage carved coral-and-jade Chinese bracelets are part of Sandy's personal collection.

Somehow calling the piece around Sandy's neck a necklace does not do justice to this exquisite turquoise, bone, and gold masterpiece personally made by Tony Duquette. This is a rare, one-of-a-kind jewel. You can learn about style, design,

NAME: Claudia Grau

OCCUPATION: mother and fashion and interior designer

SHAPE: lower figured

STYLE: Bohemian Treasure Hunter

INTENTION: "To feel really good."

INSPIRATION: "Textiles, especially their colors and textures."

PHILOSOPHY: "My body does not determine who I am."

MOTTO: "Make life a seductive treasure hunt: collect good experiences."

Claudia is constantly on the go, as a mother, a wife to a busy doctor, and an entrepreneur running a successful design business. Claudia's zest for living really informs her personal style.

"I'd wear this out to a fancy event or at a cocktail party at home," she says of this quirky ensemble. The Victorian A-line black mourning skirt with hand-sewn velvet ribbons and dramatic train looks like it came off the runway yesterday. The bustier is made with a vintage Japanese obi, proving that if what you want doesn't exist, you can create it. The jacket is 1940s wool crepe decorated with hand-hammered nail heads. The beads are black jet and the Victorian comb is tortoiseshell. This outfit conspires beautifully to give Claudia a slender, highly flattering hourglass curve.

"Live with intention. Play with abandon."

—Mary Anne Radmacher-Hershey,
American poet

CHAPTER 5

intention dressing

AT WORK

You know your shape, you know the silhouettes that suit it, and you've redis-
covered your personal style. But how
do you strut your stuff and express your
style every day? I call it intention
dressing, or expressing your style
in different ways to achieve various effects, purposes, and
desires. Clothes are powerful. Best of all, your personal
style can take you every-
where—to the office, the play-
ground, the PTA, dinner, the beach,
even for a stroll down the red carpet—
you name it! You can build a wardrobe
around your intentions. • To be clear, intention
dressing is not a particular style, as described in the
previous chapter. Rather, it describes the process of
putting together outfits thoughtfully to achieve a goal,
convey a certain idea, or even fulfill a fantasy.

You can dress for intentions regardless of whether you are, for example, a classic or a bohemian.

Once you've identified your shape and understand your silhouettes, recognizing intention is the most functional aspect of getting dressed. Dressing for the occasion, whatever it is, aids you in making strides in life. The right outfit helps you land a certain job, make a splash at a weekend pool party, seduce a paramour, intrigue new friends, or simply get noticed at the right time in the right place.

Getting Started

This chapter focuses on intention dressing for work. Chapter 6 looks at intention dressing for play. And chapter 7 looks at evening glamour and seduction dressing. There's a lot of information to absorb; these individual sections will help you achieve your goal.

Each time you get dressed, ask yourself what you are getting dressed for (work, a date, a trip to the farmer's market). And, most important, what you want to accomplish. This often-forgotten question is imperative to answer because your motives best help you determine how to express yourself through your clothes. For example, are you getting dressed for work today to make an impression at a meeting, to ask for a raise, or just to have a quiet day to get through the piles of papers on your desk? Are you going to the farmer's market in the hopes of bumping into a cute guy you saw last weekend? Are you attending a black-tie fund-raiser and planning to network? Don't stop at your motives. Ask yourself who you are dressing for. For yourself, a boyfriend, your boss? Maybe you dress for your girlfriends. Be honest. There is no wrong answer. "I dress to get attention from my friends" is a different intention than "I dress to impress my boss" or "I dress for comfort and mobility" or "I want to be famous!" or "I just like blending in."

Second, it's important to get in touch with your fantasies. Your dreams are as important as your real-life intentions and motives. Forge past your outward-directed clothing motives to focus on the ones that please you alone. Do you secretly want to be sexy and smoldering? Have you always wanted to be sassy and bold? Indulge your deepest imaginings and incorporate them into your everyday dressing schemes to further your intentions.

Clothes That Work

Maybe you feel that your work clothes leave you in a uniform rut. You're rushing to get out the door and so you fall back on the same old thing—easy to put on and requiring no thought. Or worse, you end up leaving the house with wet hair, wearing running shoes. *You just want to get to the office.* By rushing and settling for an easy "out" you are doing yourself and your career ambitions a real disservice.

I realize women work in hundreds of professions now, and many of you own your own businesses. Different jobs require different clothes. That opens up wardrobe possibilities—but working in unconventional jobs doesn't make what you wear any less important. Obviously, if you are working on a road crew or in a chocolate factory, you're dressing in sturdy denim and boots or a white coat and rubber gloves. If you're a doctor or a nurse, you're faced with some limitations. But the majority of you, who work in more conventional office settings, shouldn't settle for what's easy. Express your personality, style, and intentions every day.

Add your own spin to even the most classic professional looks; for example, a woman's white shirt with man-tailored details such as double-button cuffs and a button-down collar paired with a black skirt, or a basic black turtleneck sweater and gray pants, helps you achieve your intention

style diary

Mix Things Up!

Start with a favorite piece and build five or six updated looks around it. For example, take your best-loved jeans and sweater and try pairing them with unexpected components: try the jeans with a ruffled organza blouse or the sweater with a voile skirt. The big mix-up is a great way to get out of a style rut and breathe new life into the clothes you own.

professionally *and* stylishly. And don't forget about your personality piece (see chapter 9 for more on that) just because you're at work. Your treasured vintage pin or hand-painted scarf lightens up a staid suit or a simple shift.

If you are partial to ruffled tops, pair one with the skirt instead of wearing a white shirt, or try the classic turtleneck with Capris or ankle-length slacks and red patent-leather driving shoes. You'll see that you can mix it up and still look right for a meeting, a presentation, or a day spent at your desk.

Office dressing doesn't have to mean dull dressing. You can *feel* sexy and look professional. At a meeting you may be dressing for your boss, but you can step out of that stiff uniform look without upsetting the apple cart. A silky modern-print blouse punches up a classic blue suit and makes you feel a little seductive—but not in an overtly sexual way. There are different kinds of seductive. The feel of the fabric and the modern print give just the lift you need to approach your boss and talk him or her into giving you a plum assignment or a raise.

A bright scarf or a unique necklace adds style to a simple outfit. Even a doctor or a lawyer can add pizzazz to her look without compromising appropriateness for power. For example, a doctor might add a colorful scarf around her neck or snazzy red shoes. How else can she make her stark white lab coat individual?

Of course, you have to consider your own and others' comfort level at work. Don't dress unconsciously or impulsively. Otherwise, your outfit may backfire. For example, you forget that you have a meeting with outside clients known to be on the conservative side. Without thinking you put on a brand-new leopard-print sweater you've been dying to wear, an above-the-knee black skirt, and knee-high

boots. Any other day or with any other clients, it would be perfectly acceptable. But if your intention is to impress the old-fashioned customers, you might have blown it. Check your calendar and select clothes with your day in mind.

Like any other outfit, the work outfit has to be assembled piece by piece, with full consciousness of what you're after. Recently I was working with Shawn King (you'll see some of her favorite outfits here), helping her come up with an outfit for an important meeting. She has a perfect body and she's tall and looks good in anything. Easy job, right? Wrong.

When I arrived, Shawn was wearing a black suit and a white shirt. It really wasn't "her" at all. This is where the intention came into it. What was she trying to convey in the meeting? She is a crossover country artist—if anything, a black suit may have worked against her intentions for the meeting. If you're an artist, you want to communicate your originality, and in her case, add a little bit of country to the look.

We started with one piece, the top. The focus should be on the top for a meeting outfit because it's nearest your face. I asked her, "What top do you love? Which one makes you feel great, hot, and sexy?" If you are going to a meeting and you want to convince someone of something, you want to be on fire! She picked a nudeish, blond-colored charmeuse blouse with suede fringe. If she wore the collar open, it would have a slightly western feel, but with no *Hee-Haw* overtones. It was sophisticated. When we put a nude camisole underneath, the look started evolving. That blouse and camisole became the outfit's power center.

Beaded pants would not have been an option because they would have competed with the blouse. We went with a darker brown corduroy jean with a simple lace-up front. They kind of disappeared in a good way, to show off the top. I hope you're starting to see how to put together an outfit one piece at a time. When you think of the whole outfit, it's overwhelming. Instead, the step-by-step, trial-and-error method lets you see whether your choices are working.

Next we moved on to accessories. We tried necklaces. She needed to have a lariat. The one we chose was simple and clean. We tried a turquoise belt buckle, and it was perfect. And she had high-heeled cowboy boots that lengthened the line of the pants. We worked it right down to the bag and the earrings. Her diamond earrings felt "off," so we omitted them. We chose an Hermès Kelly bag, which became the personality piece. We wanted to put in a very classic element that also said *luxury*. A fringe bag would not have worked because it would have been too predictable. The bag conveyed another element of who she is: classy and sophisticated. Most important, she felt *great*, which was not the way she felt in her black suit. The outfit worked for her: the meeting was a success.

The process is the same for any woman who's going on a job interview, attending a meeting, or pitching an idea. Ask yourself, What aspect of myself do I want to project?

style diary

Ready, Set, Raid!

A great way to extend your wardrobe and learn about stretching the limits of basic pieces is to go on safari—in your own house (or a good friend's closet). Put on a typical work outfit, then team it with your teenager's leather motorcycle jacket. (He won't mind. If he does, he's grounded!) Wrap your husband's tie around the waistline of a black skirt. Roll the waist of your gabardine skirt and throw a chunky weekend sweater over it. Mix and match your casual Ts with silk blouses. Tuck a bright jersey tank under a staid black dress—and let the color peek out of the neckline. I promise you will find new ways of wearing work clothes and stretch your attitudes about what constitutes a professional look. Creativity is like exercise—if you don't practice it regularly, you're likely to get out of shape!

Clothes-That-Work Essentials

Basic pieces can be used to build countless looks for all your workplace intentions, and you can add unique pieces and accessories throughout the seasons. Midweight fabrics can be worn almost year-round, especially in air-conditioned offices, which seem more frigid in summer than they do in winter! I suggest seasonal options within essentials, but when it comes to basics, there are not as many as you think. It's not necessary to have two entirely separate wardrobes for spring/summer and winter/fall. Many basic pieces can cross over easily.

The essentials lists in this chapter include what I call savior pieces. If you have these items in your closet, you can put together an outfit. You can add your bohemian ethnic items or your vintage jewelry to express your style. You can transform clean-lined basics from boardroom to trendy bar easily, with accessory switches or by trading in one of the basics for a more unique item. For example, the same pants and basic knit top are transformed with the addition of a beaded blazer or a velvet wrap.

Think of these savior items as a canvas ready for your personal palette. Don't forget the Shape of Style guidelines and be sure that each item is in the right silhouette for you. Refresh your memory in chapter 3. And remember that fabrics such as wool and silk need either hand washing or dry cleaning. Refer to chapter 10 for tips on cleaning, care, and storage.

Put your personal stamp on:

Pants. Two or three pairs in shapes that flatter your figure and in neutral colors such as black, navy, or tan should do. You'll usually want to wear more formal fabrics for work, although cotton and cotton blends are certainly options for spring and summer. Otherwise, microfibers, gabardine, and twill hold up well and maintain a polished appearance from morning to quitting time in all seasons. Wool is great for fall and winter. Linen is cool, but has a tendency to wrinkle and requires so much aftercare, in terms of ironing. No matter how much starch you use, you end up looking rumpled by noon. Leave linen alone for the office. Depending on where you work, you may want to stick to classic tailored styles and flat-front pants. Drawstrings are casual look-ing (and flatter only the most linear woman). Lots of side pockets, flaps, and embellishment on work pants are probably not appropriate. Simple is better.

You can always dress up a dark trouser with a rhinestone belt if you are going out after work. Wearing rhinestone-encrusted pants to the office is very likely a no-no at your company. If glitz is your style, add some bling by replacing the pants' plain button with a crystal one.

Skirts. Skirts give you a break from wearing pants. But like essential trousers, they should be in a solid dark or neutral color that works with many tops and shoes and accessories. Lengths should flatter, but to be truly versatile, should be neither too short nor too long. Dramatic lengths (microminis or floor length) turn skirts from essential pieces to personality pieces, and such lengths may not be acceptable to your colleagues, or worse, your boss. One skirt just above and one just below the knee give the most flexibility, especially if you are planning on going from desk to date. Look for transseasonal fabrics such as twill, lightweight-wool gabardine, and cotton/poly blends. For the big chill, add heavier-weight wool pieces, but only if you live in a freezing climate. Remember, you'll be in a heated office. The same philosophy goes for summer weather. Add cotton or cotton-blend versions in warm-weather neutrals such as beige and navy. They are useful and comfortable for steamy commutes.

Shirts. You can't have too many classic white cotton and silk shirts. A finished hem is preferable. It gives you the option to wear the shirt tucked or untucked, depending on the style of your essential bottom. This hem is also flattering for all Shape of Style figures. Colored shirts, such as black, blue, or cream, can also act as essential pieces.

Knit tops. Whether classic V- or scoop-neck Ts, with short or long sleeves, simple knit tops offer so many possibilities—wear them under a sweater or a jacket, on their own, tucked in or out, embellished with a beaded choker, a scarf, or a pendant . . . and on and on. The essential knit top should fit snugly, not tightly. White, black, and navy are the most useful, of course, but colors that enhance your complexion (warm peach, sky blue, etc.) also work as essentials.

Sweaters. Cardigans are more relaxed stand-ins for blazers and jackets over shirts and knit tops or tanks, but they can also be worn as a top, buttoned up much like a shirt. Twinsets are extremely versatile because each piece can be worn on its own or together. It's worth having a winter-weight, finely knit cardigan or twinset in navy, cranberry, or basic black and a lighter silk or cotton-knit set for spring, perhaps in a lighter color. A pullover or turtleneck sweater is handy, too. Not all sweaters are basic. Sweaters with intricately knitted patterns or beading and embroidery detail are accents.

Black or brown high heels. Look for simple pumps versatile enough to be worn with pants or a skirt. A 2½-inch heel is the most multipurpose. If you're short, you can go a bit higher, and if you are tall, a lower kitten heel or a Louis heel (these curve gracefully to a narrow tip, in an S shape) gives the impression of a pump without the added stature.

Jacket. This piece must have a multiplicity of uses. The essential jacket is not the tartan plaid or the one with embroidered lapels or even a pinstripe. It's a black or cream or camel-colored jacket you wear all the time because you can style it differently every day. One-button or cardigan styles are the most universally flattering, although hourglass and linear women can wear fitted shapes. What I like about a jacket is that it's a confidence piece. You rely on it to give your top and bottom a structure and a reason for being—in short, the addition of a jacket creates an outfit.

A trench or other all-weather coat. Choose one that suits your shape and that you can throw on over pants or skirts in transitional weather.

Socks and hose. Black hose are a must-have all the way through late spring, when, if your legs are good, you can go bare. Nude stockings aren't that modern, but are useful if you don't feel comfortable going bare-legged in the summer. Trouser socks in tones that match your pants are worth stocking in multiples, since they seem to have a relatively short life span. Knee or midcalf styles are best, since you do not want a gap between the top of the sock and the bottom of the pant to show when you are seated.

NAME: Marilyn Lue

OCCUPATION: fashion stylist

SHAPE: linear

STYLE: Unconventional Elegance

INTENTION: "I do not want to look like everybody else, but I don't dress for shock value. I just want to be original."

INSPIRATION: "I get a lot of ideas from architectural elements, home design, and music."

PHILOSOPHY: "It's better to be looked over than overlooked!"

marilyn is a cosmopolitan woman who also happens to be a full-time country girl, but she never skimps on style. "I strive toward elegance, even if we're just going out to the movies as a family," says Marilyn.

For work Marilyn has to be chic but comfortable. This outfit fills the bill. The Prada skirt's unique seams play up the subtle curves of Marilyn's figure. The flared panels at the hem bring weight to the bottom of the outfit and the wooly cardigan with shawl collar balances it out. The belt is really a standout—it can be wrapped different ways, such as a stole or a collar. Marilyn's newsboy cap was made by Molly Farley. The Mont Blanc watch was originally a gift for Marilyn's husband. The driving gloves are Isotoners. A vintage brown leather envelope bag completes the look.

The graphic cashmere sweater, found at a sample sale, gives Sandy's upper body sleek structure. Pairing wool pants with metallic silver snakeskin sling backs trimmed in black gives her a long line and a tailored yet modern look. Sandy works with clients ranging from businesspeople to celebrities. "The shoes take the outfit to another level without taking it over the edge. I have to demonstrate confidence in fashion, but I can't push it because I have to assure my clients I can represent them well," she says. The Randolph Duke silver fox shrug is my own couture design. This personality piece gives the outfit its *wow* factor. Sandy unearthed vintage kid-leather gloves at a New York flea market!

Erinn's work clothes have to be comfortable and easy to wear—but also elegant with an edge, since she works in a creative environment. This chic black suit does the trick. "It's from Century 21, where I shop all the time because I live nearby. I go there for suits and basics after I drop my daughter off at school," says Erinn. The classic trench coat was scored on a trip to a Paris sample sale. "I bought the shoes in Milan on a business trip." They're cowhide with leather straps, denim insoles, and wooden heels. They give the outfit the twist that Erinn is looking for.

SHAWN Shawn is a singer, so her work wardrobe takes a completely different turn. This outfit is a showstopper! The Donna Karan black knit top has crocheted inserts running down the arms. Shawn wears two turquoise necklaces for a splash of intense color. Vivian Turner custom made the black suede wrap for her—and it's a perfect way to accentuate narrow hips and thighs. It's topped by an antique concha belt, which she found at Tracey Ross, a Sunset Strip boutique. The black leather pants are classic lace fronts from North Beach Leather. "People always ask me if these are by some groovy designer, but North Beach has never stopped making this 1960s design," she explains.

MERLE Whether she is working at home or at her office at *Harper's Bazaar,* Merle wears clothes that excite her. "If I walk out the door in an outfit I don't like, I am not going to have a good day," she says. This outfit pairs an architectural wool crepe skirt by Morgane Le Fay with a bejeweled white sweater from Balenciaga and pearls from Chanel. The black satin shoes made for dancers are new but have a vintage feel and cost only $60.

NAME: Constance White

OCCUPATION: fashion journalist and style expert; style director for eBay

SHAPE: linear

STYLE: Flashy Minimalist

INTENTION: "It combines that desire to look professional with an interest in expressing who I am."

INSPIRATION: "Good designers. Women on the street. All things African. And like many women, I am inspired by my lifestyle."

PHILOSOPHY: "Pay attention to style because it can help you get what you want, but at the same time don't overplay it. Clothes are a tool you control, not the other way around."

Constance is one of those women you turn to look at as she passes you on the street. She's stunning and regal, but totally approachable. She is immersed in fashion and style trends, but she keeps it simple and clean with a little bit of glamour thrown in so she (and we) won't get bored.

Here, the blue/black wool skirt comes from a controversial late 1990s collection by Jean Paul Gaultier. The attached belt with metal buckle adds interest and creates the illusion of hips. The bag is calfskin, and her jewelry includes an Elsa Peretti link bracelet. "My husband gave it to me; I wear it all the time," she says.

TOBI   As an interior designer juggling several projects, Tobi has to look good but still be comfortable enough to go from construction site to client meeting to dinner date. This all-white outfit fills the bill beautifully—and it's very L.A. She wrapped the simple shirt instead of buttoning it, which creates the illusion of a curvy waist. The aviator sunglasses are hip, the handbag is a signature bag from YSL (Yves Saint-Laurent), the belt is silver and leather. "I tied my hair back with a scarf. It's sleek, chic, and practical," she says.

CHERYL   Cheryl is busy running her skin care line, developing new businesses, and modeling. "I would wear this to a meeting. The beaded top is spectacular and surprising. Worn with a long black skirt it would be black tie," she says. The curve-enhancing jacket and boots add to the look's tailored elegance. "Women would get a kick out of it—and men would be bowled over by it," she says. Off her face but still long, Cheryl's simple hairstyle is both practical and glamorous—just like Cheryl. The antique earrings further add to the outfit's understated glamour.

TAMARA   "Because I work in the fashion business, where there is no strict dress code, I don't have to wear a smart suit every day. Our office is very creative," Tamara says of her work style. While Tamara loves color, she's also very minimal. Case in point, this multihued coat by Missoni, "This coat is very comfy; you can throw it over jeans or a skirt," says Tamara. The fabric's weave, along with the belted waist and traditional placket at the top, creates interest and keeps the eye moving on a linear shape.

The cream bag is soft and slouchy leather. The Jimmy Choo sandals are dark braided leather. "I don't like to match shoes and bags," the entrepreneur says. Simple black sunglasses add a little mystery to the package.

107

"I have often said that I wish I had invented blue jeans: the most **SPECTACULAR**, the most **PRACTICAL**, the most **RELAXED** and **NONCHALANT**. They have **EXPRESSION**, **MODESTY**, **SEX APPEAL**, **SIMPLICITY**— all I hope for in my clothes."

—Yves Saint-Laurent, clothing designer

CHAPTER 6

intention dressing

AT PLAY

Casual clothes, weekend wear, and vacation attire offer the most opportunity to express yourself freely. The downside is that many of us get lazy and pull on sweatpants and a T without really thinking through the options. Remember to keep it neat: "casual" and "slob" are not interchangeable. Here's where you can have some fun! You can really be fearless and free during downtime. • If every woman could travel the world—Asia, Africa, Italy--and see herself in different ways, through the eyes of different cultures, then she would learn that she can mix an Indian sari with a pair of jeans or put on an Italian knit dress with a pile of African necklaces. That's the way a lot of trendsetters dress today, especially when it comes to casual.

The individualist takes a great straw bag she picked up in the islands, pairs it with gingham pants from a department store, and tops it all off with an embroidered peasant blouse bought in Mexico and espadrilles imported from Spain.

A casual look like the one described above is so much more satisfying to put together and fun to wear to a barbecue or a brunch than the same old dungaree shorts or yoga pants and tank top. If you can't travel to find unusual items, check out import clothing stores and the Internet. I have been in the smallest towns and found boutiques that sell unique clothes from around the world. And the Internet has no boundaries. Both options are great ways to bring the world to your doorstep.

Don't say, "I couldn't possibly" when contemplating a certain look. This is the time to play and experiment. If there's a secret desire or you really love it, try it. It may seem like there are "fashion police" on every corner nowadays, but daring to follow your fashion fantasies is not against the law yet. You will not get arrested!

Since downtime encompasses so many activities—from reading the Sunday paper in bed to meeting friends for brunch to shopping or going to the movies to stretching out on the beach—you'll probably have more casual clothing than any other category in your closet, including work and evening.

If you engage in a specific sport, like tennis, golf, or skiing, the options are even more varied. I don't go into dressing for particular sports here, but do keep in mind that while some activities require exacting attire, you can add your personality to whatever garb is required. Just look at the famous tennis-playing Williams sisters, Venus and Serena. They don't let old-fashioned ideas about tennis togs stop them from expressing their style—and it doesn't interfere with their winning game.

However, there are two casual garments I spend some time exploring in depth later in this chapter. They are jeans, because we wear them all the time, and bathing suits, because there is a great deal of anxiety surrounding them.

Clothes-at-Play Essentials

Casual clothes offer a chance to experiment with fashion and fantasy. Since your intention is most likely to relax and have fun—maybe meet new people, flirt, or kick back with friends—you can go out on a limb and try something new.

Essentials are a base from which to express your style within the casual vernacular, especially if you are just beginning to experiment. For example, if you already like bohemian style, you might as well start with the basics and build on them. You never go wrong with a black turtleneck or great-fitting pants, which you can translate into a bohemian look with ethnic flats, hippie beads, or an embroidered shawl from the Middle East. You can always feminize, personalize, and embellish basics to match your intention.

Jeans. You need two or three great-fitting pairs (see the jeans section in this chapter for much more information).

Fitted sweaters. Choose two or three in a solid color and in a neck style that flatters you (turtle, V, scoop, etc.). To give the sweater more flexibility, be sure it fits sleekly through the torso but is not so tight that you can't fit a tank, a camisole, or even a lightweight button-down shirt underneath. Have at least two sweaters on hand in spring- or summer-weight cotton or silk knits and two in heavier cashmere, wool, or angora or a blend for fall and winter. The Fair Isle knit or fisherman's knits are not basic sweaters— fancy or ethnic knits are an outfit's defining feature. They don't stay in the background.

T-shirts. Make sure you have a selection of lightweight, fine-gauge jersey T-shirts with short and long sleeves, as well as sleeveless and tank styles. Each can be layered under and over other T-shirts, or worn under sweaters, shirts, and jackets, depending on the season. Of course, they work on their own in warmer weather.

Great white cotton shirts. A straight hem gives you the option of wearing it in or out. The casual white shirt can be the same as your work shirt— and do double duty. Or you can have casual versions, in softer cottons. For example, you might have polished cotton shirts for 9 to 5 use and softer linens and washed cottons for weekend wear. Linen shirts have a tendency to wrinkle, so reserving them for weekend activities like flea marketing or as a cover-up après beach makes sense. You are not so concerned about wrinkles, and a slightly rumpled look works in these circumstances. It gives your outfit a pleasing throwaway ease (just make sure everything else you're wearing is not wrinkled, or you'll end up looking like an unmade bed).

Denim jacket or leather bomber.

A great black dress. Choose a simple one that you can completely personalize to your liking and dress up or down depending on the event.

Pants. You need a versatile pair that you can wear with many different tops and that flatters your figure, in cotton, twill, or a casual microfiber. Casual pants are most versatile in black, navy, or chocolate for fall; lighter neutrals, such as cream, taupe, or army green, work better for spring.

Great flat shoes. These can be an assortment of sneakers, one pair of driving shoes, loafers, mules, thong sandals, or any low heels that gets you around all year and that are comfortable worn with or without socks.

Boots. Preferably, these should coordinate with all of your casual outfits, such as a black or brown leather in a lower heel of choice—consider stacked and chunky or a midheel. The boots can be knee-high or ankle length, or midcalf. Knee-highs look best with skirts; other boot heights look best when worn under pants.

Bathing suits. Everyone has to have at least one and preferably two comfortable bathing suits that fit and perform in and out of the water.

Socks. Stock up on multiple pairs of cotton and trouser socks in colors that blend with your pants. Remember the caveat about "the gap"—midcalf and knee-high socks are best. As soon as the weather is warm enough, try aban-

workout about wear

Working out, aside from being the best way to stay in shape, often puts you in a social situation. No matter what you do, whether it's working the machines at a local gym, going for a run or a walk in your neighborhood, or taking classes at a Pilates or yoga studio, you want to look neat and put together. I live in Los Angeles, so I certainly see some glitzy outfits at Hollywood gyms. But I hesitate to put too much emphasis on getting dressed to go to the gym. If the thought of getting decked out to exercise discourages you from getting out there and moving, forget it. Wear what's comfortable and get going. Clothing worn for exercise is insignificant when compared to the health benefits of activity.

For most women the guidelines are pretty simple: workout clothes should be in good condition (get rid of anything torn or stained), comfortable, and easy to move in. Low-rise flared-leg yoga pants are fantastic for all shapes and are comfortable to work out in—have a few on hand for wash and wear. These pants are available in 100 percent cotton and Lycra-cotton blends. Basic T-shirts or tank tops, a couple of sweatshirts, and a good pair of athletic shoes, appropriate for your chosen sport, are all you really need to complete your workout wardrobe. If you have long hair, it's a good idea to pull it back with a fabric-covered rubber band. If you're heading outdoors, don't forget the sunscreen, lip balm, and shades!

doning socks with slip-on shoes—it's a more stylish, modern look. You can make an exception when wearing sneakers. If you're doing a lot of running around, white cotton anklets keep your feet comfortable, cool, and dry.

You'll notice I omitted the skirt as an essential in the casual category. I think it's an option for casual wear, but it serves as more of a mood setter or a personality piece. Use the power of a unique skirt for casual times to make a sexy, flirty, or unconventional point or to feminize a very tailored look. For example, a cotton mini or a long gauzy peasant skirt paired with a T is a very different look than the same T with jeans or shorts—even if you keep the basic accessories the same.

Jeans: The Ultimate Go-To Piece

Jeans are in a class and category by themselves. Denim is timeless and completely modern. I don't see it ever going away. And you can wear jeans no matter what your age. If you have a great-looking pair that fits you, worn with a fabulous cashmere sweater, boots, a jacket, and a stylish haircut, you'll look elegant, especially as an older woman. My mother wears her jeans this way and she looks terrific.

You can't have too many jeans, either. I have three pairs in three different washes and I rotate them. One is grayish, one is darker and tailored, and one is a very papery, blue denim color. It makes sense to have more than one pair of jeans: one for casual weekend wear, one that can be worn to work, and one that is frankly seductive and good for evening.

What's thrilling about jeans is the mix of ideas you can achieve with them. They serve as a backdrop for other clothes, and it's exciting to play off of the high-low aspect of jeans dressing. A ruffled blouse or tuxedo jacket, great jewels, and high heels create a *wow* evening outfit. And you can't ignore the "hip factor," either. Jeans are the ultimate power piece in the right cut and fit, and they make you hip and cool—plain and simple. Top dressing is simple with jeans: a tiny T, a lace camisole, a crisp white shirt, a silky tunic, or a sequined top—each looks beautiful with denim.

Another admirable quality of denim jeans is that they disappear. They are urban *and* suburban camouflage. Jeans are the common denominator: we all have them. If I am going to a bar for a cocktail, I like to put on my favorite jeans with a great shirt—the jeans are safe, like a soft piece of armor. Once they're on, you can forget them.

Fit and Function

Let's face it: jeans are about sex. They may have originally been designed as utilitarian work clothes, but since the late 1950s and certainly since the 1960s, women's jeans are worn everywhere, for every reason—least of which is for manual labor and most of which is about sexiness. To make sure you're prepped for a sexy look, check out your butt in the mirror. I'm serious! What I mean by that is make sure the jeans fit right and hug your bottom in the most flattering way. If the jeans really flatter your body on the bottom, the look will always work.

That said, there are a very small number of women who can't wear jeans. If you have a very flat behind, they may not be the best thing for you. On the other hand, you can wear jeans with behind enhancers, which literally pad your fanny (they are found at specialty lingerie stores and online). Another trick is to find a cut with a lot going on in that area, such as decorative pockets and stitching to deceive the eye into thinking there's more of you back there. Denim skirts are a great alternative to jeans if you have a hard time finding the right fit in pants.

Finding the perfect jeans is a very personal process. Follow the same general Shape of Style Silhouette guidelines for pants—but you need to put some extra effort into your selection. You always have to try on jeans to get the right fit. For example, how low do you go? The best way to tell? Bend over! If your crack shows, it's too low. No one wants to see it all. You don't want your thong sticking out of the top of your pants! At any rate, low rise may not flatter you, but a dropped waist may be quite becoming.

I tend to think that low-rise jeans emphasize wide hips, so be careful if you are lower figured or even an hourglass. If you are upper figured, pocket, front-placket, and side-seam detailing brings balance to your shape. If you are linear figured, go lower on the waistline; a hip hugger creates the waist-to-hip curve you are after. Waist-high jeans are difficult for most women to wear, unless they are balanced with a flared or boot-cut leg.

style diary

You're a Jean-ius

How many different looks can you create with your favorite pair of jeans? Take out an array of tops, belts, jewelry, and shoes. Pull on your jeans and see what you come up with. Challenge yourself to create three looks each for work, daytime, and evening.

It's wise to buy your jeans a bit snug because they always stretch out; the knees, waist, and back of the pants end up sagging after a while. Start with a slightly smaller pair, which stretches to conform to your body, but doesn't end up being baggy.

As with standard tailored pants, the boot-cut leg is the most flattering type. It's also trendier and more current than straight-cut legs. But just like trousers or khakis, you can find jeans that are pegged, cropped, and bell-bottomed. Waists can be high, low, or hip hugging.

> ## "Blue jeans are the most beautiful things since the gondola."
>
> —Diana Vreeland,
> former editor in chief of *Vogue*

And here's one of my few rules: jeans really need back pockets. Pockets help everyone look better—they are a miracle optical illusion. Pocket placement is important, too: pockets placed too wide make hips look wider. If pockets get placed too far from the center seam, they also look out of balance. Better to look for pockets that are centered on each side or slightly closer to the center seam.

Style and Substance

There is no such thing as too much detail, especially when it comes to jeans. But they have to be really *great* details. Look for beautiful stitching, unusual front closers (lace-ups, snaps, buttons, and, of course, the classic zipper), and interesting pocket treatments.

I'm torn about all the holes in some of today's jean styles! The truth is you don't want to look dirty at work or at a special occasion, even if it's a casual one. If jeans are too ripped or overtreated, you end up looking messy. One way to tell if the details are bad: if your eye keeps going to that hole or patch or bleached-out spot, it's not the right thing. A pair of jeans that's a personality piece, with beading or fringe up and down the side, is another story, of course. But even those special details should be a part of the entire impact of the jeans.

When wearing denim on the top as well as on the bottom, it's preferable to keep the two denims in different washes and tones. For example, wear a dark jacket with light jeans. Or try very dark jeans with a bleached denim shirt. Wear a colored denim jacket (red, orange, etc.) with blue jeans. The more mismatched, the better. If the denim matches, it looks a bit like you're going to a rodeo (and if you *are* going to a rodeo, well then, go for the match).

In the end, I think one piece of denim at a time is the best way to go. Jeans look better paired with a suede, wool, or khaki jacket or blazer than they do with a denim jacket.

Bathing Beauties

I began my fashion career designing swimwear, so I know how women feel about bathing suits. It's a love-hate relationship. Swimsuits cause so much anxiety among women that even shopping for one can be a traumatic experience, let alone wearing one in front of other people at the beach or the pool. Complicating matters is the fact that a pretty, sexy bathing suit on the beach can turn into an embarrassing nightmare when you hit the water. Once wet, it can bag, sag, shrink, or, worst of all, fall off.

The Big Shop

If you are interested in swimming or playing water sports (polo, anyone?), I recommend a one-piece suit. Ditto if there is a chance that your office party, outing, or company picnic will be held at the seashore or poolside (it happens). A one-piece suit is as "professional" as a bathing suit can be.

If you are wearing a bikini, you definitely want to get up off your towel or chaise and take a stroll down the sandy shore or around the pool deck to show yourself off. Why else wear one if not to strut your stuff? Even the tiniest bikini should have sturdy ties and clasps, be lined smoothly with no puckers, and be constructed of high-quality material. Specialty suits such as crocheted styles are not really meant to get wet— these suits are about fashion and sex. They should fit securely and sit smoothly against your skin. There's nothing sexy about an ill-fitting garment of any kind, and that includes swimsuits.

A Swimming Shape of Style

Every woman can find a bathing suit that flatters her shape. Take the plunge and try some of the styles recommended here—you will be pleasantly surprised at what the right bathing suit does for your figure.

Linear-figured women create curves with a one-piece suit with high-cut legs. A belted waistline gives the appearance of a whittled middle, as does a wrapped top that forms a V-neck. Two-toned suits, with the colors running top to bottom vertically or with a bold print on top and any dark tone on the bottom, make straight figures appear curvy. Low-cut backs that end in a V are flattering. Look for one-piece suits with lace or mesh inserts. Bikinis with hip details such as side rings, ruffles, bows, and even short skirts flatter. Avoid solid-colored tank suits, high-cut necklines, and vertical stripes.

Hourglass women flatter curves with a one-piece suit with a wrap front, wide shoulder straps, square necklines, and V-necks and low-cut backs. Also try colorful print bikinis with a modified bottom that lies right below your belly button or sits high on the hip and that has hip accents such as ties, belts, or sashes. Avoid high-necked tank suits and low, straight-across bikini bottoms.

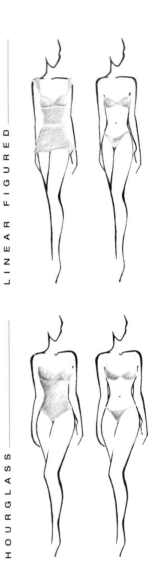

LINEAR FIGURED

HOURGLASS

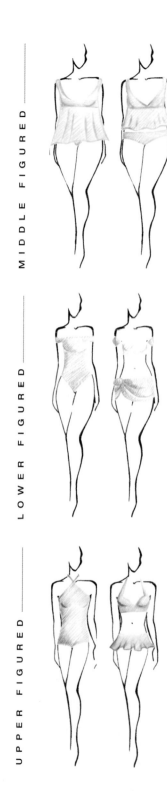

Middle-figured women benefit from one-piece suits with a built-in control panel. A one-piece wrap-front suit is also pretty, as is a maillot style with bows, crochet inserts, or neck details such as metal rings. Tankinis, two-piece suits with a tank top that meets or slightly covers the top of the bottom piece of the suit, also flatter. Try bold, large prints. Think twice about traditional bikinis and solid-colored tank style one-piece suits.

Lower-figured women look great in miniskirt two-piece suits, especially those that sit slightly lower than the belly button or right at the waist. Consider simple styles and think twice about frills or other details on the lower half of the suit. One-piece suits with details at the top are very pretty—consider ruffles, lace inserts, or decorative straps. Tops with some padding or an underwire bring balance to your figure. A bikini or a two-piece with a ruffled top flatters. For two-pieces, a high-waist bottom and a string bikini top with triangular cups is a good option. Think twice about short-style bottoms and solid-colored tank-style one-piece suits and low-cut backs.

Upper-figured women need some extra assistance on top; built-in support bras with underwires help. Halter-style tops also offer support and provide sexy cleavage. Look for halters that are banded around the midriff and can be tied in back and around the neck. Straight-cut bust styles such as a classic tank in a solid color minimize a large bust. Wide shoulder straps are more comfortable and accommodating than thin spaghetti straps. Short styles and skirted styles bring balance to the shape. Think twice about strapless bandeau tops and triangular string bikini tops.

NAME: Tobi Tobin

OCCUPATION: interior designer and novelist (*Door to Door*)

SHAPE: middle figured

STYLE: Rich Rocker

INTENTION: "To convey a look of clean, sophisticated monochromatic lines I call symmetrical sexiness."

INSPIRATION: "The fashion world, good tailoring, and master fashion designers like Randolph."

PHILOSOPHY: "Accessories, accessories, accessories!"

MOTTO: "Keep it simple. It's about you, not the clothes."

tobi is worldly and very chic. She grew up in Michigan but has lived in New York City, Paris, and Los Angeles and has settled on Malibu—for the time being. A former model, she knows how to choose clothes that accentuate her assets. Even though Tobi loves fashion-forward items, there's something very timeless about her overall look because she chooses a lot of classic silhouettes.

Tobi doesn't mind transforming an item herself if it doesn't meet her needs. "This jacket was absolutely plain so I bought a border of crystal beading and attached it to the jacket." Under the jacket she wears a satin camisole and vintage lace blouse, creating the illusion of a slim waist. The vintage necklaces and silver snakeskin shoes reference the sparkle in her jacket.

SHAWN "I'd wear this outfit to dinner with friends or to a concert," says Shawn of this Coco Chanel–inspired ensemble. "It's about fun." The jacket is Chanel and has matching pants and skirt. "I don't wear Chanel all the time, but it has a place in my closet. I wear it full on or with jeans, as in this outfit," she says. The costume pearls are a mixture of different pieces from different eras.

MERLE Merle doesn't wear jeans, but that doesn't mean denim isn't at home in her closet. Since Merle is an hourglass, she can pull off this Marc Jacobs gathered skirt. "I like its volume. It's a different use for denim," she says. Her favorite piece of clothing is the linen-and-cotton-blend Rochas jacket. "I wear it with everything," says Merle. Pairing the designer jacket with casual denim creates a pleasing high-low style tension.

CLAUDIA Claudia paired her jeans with an Indian tie-dyed top she discovered in a boutique on New York City's Upper West Side. Beads, shells, and embroidery embellish its neckline. Claudia's necklaces are from her natural-coral jewelry collection. Her friend jewelry designer Hillary Bean created the intricate turquoise bracelet and freshwater kashi pearl earrings. The long top floats over Claudia's hips.

NAME: Tamara Mellon

OCCUPATION: cofounder and president, Jimmy Choo

SHAPE: linear

STYLE: International Lux

INTENTION: "To feel comfortable and always dressed in my own personal style."

INSPIRATION: "Travel inspires me the most; looking at the traditions in clothing, jewelry, architecture, music, art, and interiors of very rich cultures. For example, I take a lot of inspirational fashion trips to Istanbul and other cities in Turkey."

PHILOSOPHY: "Don't worry about following trends. You can always update an old outfit with new accessories."

CHERYL Cheryl is tall and slim, so she looks great in fitted jeans. The Randolph Duke tweedy knit jacket with fur trim has a bit of "bling." She put a basic brown $5 tank top underneath. The belt is a very long necklace tied in the back with a pretty cord. The shoes inspired this creative twist on the belt—they are covered with turquoise and add color, which Cheryl loves, to the neutral color palette. "I wear this outfit to the office or lunch with friends," says Cheryl.

t amara Mellon is a showstopper. Her classic English beauty may have you thinking "frosty"—but you'd be wrong. Her warm, throaty laugh, easy smile, and sense of humor banish those thoughts *immediately.* Tamara is a jet-setter—constantly looking for design inspiration for her company, Jimmy Choo. She's also a busy mom, so she really wants to feel comfortable but chic.

"This outfit is very simple, but it is dressed up by the necklace from the sixties," she says. Tamara's True Religion low-rise jeans in deep indigo are paired with a simple white tank and a black fox bolero-style vest. Note how the various lines and planes of the outfit create soft curves and show off her figure

NAME: Sandra Graham

OCCUPATION: publicist, fashion consultant, owner of SJB Vintage & Couture, and jewelry style director of eBay

SHAPE: middle figured

STYLE: Manhattan Chic

INTENTION: "To be anything but superficial—I want to feel happy in my clothes."

INSPIRATION: "New York City inspires me every day. Also, individualists like Millicent Rogers, Frida Kahlo, and the little old lady who sits in front of me in church with a tiger lily in her bun."

PHILOSOPHY: "Peace and confidence. You can have a closet full of designer clothes, but it's hard to pull off true personal style if you don't feel good about who you are."

MOTTO: "Don't be limited by anyone's preconceived ideas of style."

even if you've just met her, Sandy is one of those rare people you feel you've known all your life. She makes everyone who enters her world feel welcome.

Sandy's straight-leg jeans are very dark denim. The Mediterranean blue crushed-velvet top is lavishly embroidered. A vintage gold leather handbag (a birthday gift from me) and a yellow Lucite vintage ring from the '60s complete this funky look.

ERINN This Look at Me jeans outfit is somewhat unusual for Erinn. "I don't usually wear clothes this bold, but once in a while, it's fun," she says. The Marc Jacobs top is festooned with giant gems. "The funky rhinestones really made it me,"

MARILYN "I wear jeans often, since I live in the country," declares Marilyn. In this case, Marilyn paired the jeans with a vintage pony-skin coat. She l ayered a sleeveless knit tank, which features an olive green cross and a blue background,

CONSTANCE Constance keeps it simple when in jeans. The Camp Beverly Hills T is young and fresh. "I would wear these jeans to work because they are so dark and dressy and the fabric holds its shape," says Constance of her Adriano

"Our intention creates our reality."

—Wayne Dyer, author and motivator

intention dressing

GLAMOUR AND SEDUCTION

The red carpet has been pulled out from under us! What does black tie mean for a woman these days, anyway? For men, it's still fairly straightforward: a tuxedo or a very formal suit. Women have a lot more latitude: you can wear a long gown, but you don't have to. Black velvet pants with a top encrusted with jewels or an embroidered or brocade jacket is acceptable, as is a short dress in a formal fabric such as chiffon, crepe, or silk charmeuse. • The fact is, dressy clothes are the same clothes you love the rest of the time; they're just amplified and polished. Dressing up is about fabric, texture, glimmer, extravagance, and luxury. That's the impression you want to make—it doesn't have to cost a lot of money.

There's also no reason to depart from your personal preferences or the shapes that are right for your style. I've dressed so many Hollywood women and gotten them ready to walk down the red carpet—and I can tell you, it's equal parts attitude and confidence, carriage and posture, and clothes.

If you aren't the charity-ball type and don't attend events calling for fancy dress very often, you may find yourself stuck for something great to wear when such occasions do arise. And there are times when you will want to get dressed up just for the fun of it. If you train your eye, you can spot things that work for evening and can double as your personality piece: the vintage beaded purse you find at the flea market; a red taffeta bolero jacket you picked up at a designer consignment store; silk palazzo pants bought at a resort where you vacationed; a sari wrap you found from a street vendor while on lunch hour. These sorts of items add real substance and personal style to very basic evening pieces—but you can only find them if you are looking. I encourage you to always keep an eye out for pieces that could work for your evening look whenever and *wherever* you're shopping. You can never go back and find that one-of-a-kind piece you saw yesterday. It's never there. If you love it, buy it when you see it!

I want you to mix things up for evening, and that includes using pieces from your day wardrobe. The rules of when to wear day or night pieces have all but been banished. Use a beaded top with jeans for evening and a tuxedo jacket with a lace camisole and cropped pants for day. Ethnic accessories add intrigue and style and draw others to you. Items such as a Moroccan amulet, a Venetian glass bead necklace, Roman coin earrings, carved-wood-and-antique-ivory African bracelets, Native American turquoise jewelry, an embroidered Indian wrap, or a Japanese kimono add mystery and sophistication to the clean lines of modern dressing. Even basic pieces you've worn to work can be magically transformed into evening accessories with bravado and dash. For example, your black pants go glam with beaded mules and a velvet tank. A simple skirt goes red carpet when paired with a satin bustier.

Don't be afraid to employ the seduction of lingerie to create glamour. A lace camisole peeking out of a deep V-necked dress, a cashmere sweater, or a jacket, or a lace or satin slip under a soft, flirty chiffon skirt or a pleated skirt, can be unexpected and very effective in giving your evening look just the *wow* you have been hoping for!

If you are switching from office to evening and you are wearing a suit, remove your shirt and replace it with a satin-and-pearl-trimmed teddy and let it and a little skin show. With high heels and supersheer hose, you've created instant allure! Fancy jewelry adds impact to simple silhouettes, too. Think about a black satin sheath with a low back, your hair pinned up or combed away from your face. All you need are gorgeous "diamond" drop earrings and you've got it made. Or maybe you turn a workday navy knit top and pants into dinner party drama with an outrageous beaded bag and sexy embossed leather stilettos.

red carpet ready: cut yourself in half

A great way to elongate and slim the body when wearing a long gown (or any outfit, for that matter) is to drape a shawl made of a fluid fabric over your shoulder so it falls down one half of your body. You'll create the illusion of a dramatically slimmer, taller silhouette.

129

Dressing Up Essentials

You don't need a lot of evening and dressy clothes. A few essentials that have multiple uses can create many very different looks, especially if you have a cache of unusual accessories.

A great black dress. Choose one in a more formal fabric and with a sexier-than-daytime neckline. A basic V- or scoop neck in your Shape of Style Silhouette in satin, silk, or velvet, even polished cotton, is versatile. A dress like this is a good investment you can rely on for several years. It won't go out of style if you constantly update it with new accessories. If you can afford it, buy one in a summer-weight fabric, such as silk or cotton, that is sleeveless or short sleeved, and have another in a winter-weight fabric, such as wool or a wool and silk blend.

Black velvet or satin pants. These are so versatile because you can "top dress" pants with unique blouses and shells made from lace, brocade, or silk. Beaded and embroidered tops and those with ruffles, rhinestones, pearl buttons, and other similar details turn pants outfits from simple to swanky.

High heels. Stilettos and narrow-heeled shoes always look fancy, formal, and sexy. Strappy high-heeled sandals in dressy materials such as satin, metallic leather, and patent leather are also great to have on hand.

Simple black satin bag. I am partial to a plain clutch that can be changed, especially if you don't have a lifestyle that requires lots of nights out on the town (and therefore lots of different bags). A glittering brooch, silk flower, satin ribbon, and other embellishments transform one black bag into several different options. However, if you love fancy or vintage evening bags, go ahead and collect them. A great little beaded or embroidered bag can be your outfit's focal point.

Sheer black hose. Dark, sheer stockings, especially those with an added bit of sheen, are sexy and help a short skirt or dress look red-carpet ready.

style diary

Often a formal occasion or event is thrown at you unexpectedly and you find your-self at a department store buying something "appropriate" or "okay" that you really don't like at all. And it usually ends up costing an arm and a leg. Instead of being caught off guard and unprepared for special events, take time now to put together a few evening looks with items you have or can dress up with easy-to-find new accessories. How many evening looks can you create? What pieces are missing from your wardrobe? What can you add? What items can you put together in unex-pected ways to shake up a basic dress or skirt and top for evening occasions?

Have a Ball Gown

Even though I don't think having evening gowns on hand is necessary for the majority of women, I absolutely love the glamour of them. That's the main reason I adore designing red-carpet looks. Gowns are pure fantasy—you can be the fairy princess you've always wanted to be. If you do have an event coming up that allows you to wear a long dress, you can do one of two things, and both have merit.

The first option is to invest in a simple gown that can be transformed in different ways so it looks fresh enough to wear numerous times. Let the accessories lead the way. However, if you want to make a splash and it's a very special occasion (like your wedding or the Academy Awards), then go all out and choose something with remarkable details such as beading or embroidery. The dress does the talking in this situation.

Evening gowns, whether simple and chic or ornamental and elabo-rate, are made in basic silhouettes. Here are the shapes that are right for your figure:

Middle figured: To flatter, choose a dress that skims the waistline and continues into a floor-length A-line. Empire-waist dresses are very glamorous, as is a slightly fitted shift with bust darts and a V- or scoop neck. Look for embellishments (beads, crystals, etc.) at the neckline and hem. Think twice about halter-topped gowns and those with a seam or a belt detail at the waistline, a fitted bodice, a gathered pouf skirt, or a low-cut back. All emphasize thicker middles.

Lower figured: To flatter, try gowns cut on the bias and A-line skirts with fitted tops. Jersey wrap gowns are also pretty, including those with plunging necklines that show some cleavage. Low-cut backs are sexy, especially if you love your behind and want to show it off. Mermaid styles that fit and flare at the bottom are also appealing. Look for details and embellishments at the neckline and hem. Think twice about halter-style dresses, anything too fitted and straight on the bottom, or Empire-waist gowns, which make you look larger.

Hourglass: To flatter, go for wrap dresses, fitted shifts, bias-cut gowns with flared skirts, and mermaid styles. Plunging necklines and backs are also pretty, as are backless halter dresses. Look for embellishments at the neck, back, and hem. Think twice about loose-fitting styles, muumuus, Empire waists, and prints with horizontal lines.

Linear figured: To flatter, a belted gown creates the illusion of a waist, as do wrap dresses; bias-cut and fit-and-flare styles also work. Look for embellishment at the waist, neckline, and hips. Strapless dresses with sweetheart necklines create a pretty bustline. Think twice about boxy or straight-cut styles, prints with horizontal lines, straight-across strapless necklines, tube-style gowns, and clingy knit dresses that emphasize straight lines.

Upper figured: To flatter, choose bias-cut, A-line, and lightly fitted sheath styles. Mermaid dresses also flatter. Think twice about strapless dresses, Empire waists, cinched waists, and slim-fitting knits.

Turn It On—Dressing for Seduction

There are many forms of dressing for seduction, largely because we all have very different ideas about what we find sexy and enticing. So first and foremost, figure out what makes your object of desire's pulse race. Let that

grandillusion

If you don't want to show too much skin but still want to feel sexy, consider choosing dresses that have long or short sleeves and backs and shoulder areas made of illusion fabric. It is a sheer, fine-mesh material that offers coverage and a hint of flesh without exposing too much skin. Also remember that reflective fabrics like satin and charmeuse, and metallic finishes, especially when made into fitted dresses, all add weight. If you don't want to add visual pounds, stick to matte-finish fabrics or those that don't have too much shine. If you absolutely love the look and feel of shiny satin, look for a dress that uses that fabric as trim to convey the feeling of sheen.

be your cue when dressing for seduction. People react to different visual stimuli. Some men love lacy, sexy underthings on women—that's the cliché. I always think of the Hugh Grant character in the first Bridget Jones movie—he was absolutely nuts for Bridget's "granny pants." You can't predict what turns people on!

Second, you have to ask yourself, What is it I'm trying to convey? What do I want to happen? Do you want to entice a first date so he comes back for seconds? Or are you ready to make a major move with a heartthrob you've been seeing for a while? Each of these situations requires a different look. For a first date, you may want to be sexy but a bit demure and show a touch of cleavage by leaving one extra button on a silk blouse undone but pair the top with jeans and sexy leather boots. In the latter case, you might consider going all out with a plunging neckline, a skirt with a thigh-high slit, and stilettos.

Third, *you* have to feel seductive in the clothes you wear. If you feel silly, exposed, or uncomfortable, you're not going to be seducing anyone anytime soon. Authenticity is so important because the reality is—more often than not—sexier than the fakery.

But feeling a little naughty or risqué is not a bad thing, so take a deep breath and unbutton one more button.

Think silks and cashmere, which are both very sensual. What feels sexy to you? It may not be the predictable "romantic" items such as black lace panties or a satin teddy. Even the most conservative suit you have can become lethal with some killer stilettos and a provocatively unbuttoned shirt.

The whole point of seduction dressing is to look alluring, approachable, and fresh. At the end of the day, if seduction is your object, the clothes are all coming off anyway. But the only way to feel sexy when you're in front of someone else is to get used to feeling that way when you're alone.

Take a quiet morning or afternoon and try on your prettiest slips, camisoles, bras (you know, the stuff you're saving for a special occasion—guess what? It's arrived!). Walk around in them; get used to feeling your body move in sexy clothing. Try unbuttoning a shirt to show some cleavage. Put on some tight jeans with heels—and just be. The senses play a large part in seduction. Posture and posturing in general make a big difference. Get in touch with your body and be conscious of the way it feels to be in sexy clothes.

If your lower body is not what you want it to be and you have great shoulders, play them up with a silky top that's sliding off one shoulder or toss a sweater over the shoulder, especially if you're wearing a twinset.

style diary

The Great Black Dress Project

What can you do with a simple black dress? How many intentions can you fulfill with it? How would you wear it for work? With a cardigan tied around your shoulders and some heels. For weekends? Throw a denim jacket over it. For evening? It's all about one great pair of high-heeled sandals. What about seduction? Hey, maybe it's your outfit left draped over your dressing table chair. . . . How would you make the black dress edgy? Maybe you wear it over woodblock print pants. A basic like a black dress stretches your imagination and helps you see new connections between your accessories.

If you have a great bust, try different kinds of tops and observe their effects. I like tops that look like they are about to fall off (but don't actually, until you want them to). Most men find that alluring. A little lingerie or a pretty bra strap peeking out from under a blouse or a sweater is very inviting.

If you feel insecure about your middle section, wear something that camouflages it and play up something you love, perhaps your legs. Legs typically turn men on. This largely has to do with what is antithetically male. That's why guys love strappy sandals. There's nothing androgynous about a high heel.

If you don't feel your body is your asset, go with what you have. It's the law of the jungle—use every asset at your disposal. If your best feature is your smile, concentrate on your lipstick. Make your mouth and smile the focus of your look and use them to seduce. Eyes are an important tool for seduction, so play them up. Consider a little smoky eye shadow and individually applied eyelashes—killer! Let your hair down or at least loosen it up, especially after work. Play with it and muss it a little using your fingertips. (There's more on hair and makeup in chapter 10.)

Seductive Essentials: Get Comfortable with Your Sensual Side

It's nearly impossible to list items that are "essential" for seductive dressing. It's more important—well, *essential*—to be comfortable in your skin. But here are a few items that help you create a seductive feeling:

1. Bras and panties in a style that makes you feel hot, and maybe just a bit giddy or nervous.
2. Jeans that make you feel sexy—at least one pair.
3. A sexy sweater, maybe something that reveals your shoulders.
4. High heels.
5. A "postseduction" white shirt for tossing on the morning after.

Once you have the essentials for each category of your life—work, play, glamour occasions, and seduction—you can create an outfit for any intention or purpose. I urge you to cross-pollinate the essentials—mix your seductive pieces with your work clothes, casual with formal. Stretch the limits.

NAME: Erinn Williams

OCCUPATION: video production company owner

SHAPE: hourglass

STYLE: Classic Modern Vintage

INTENTION: "To highlight my strengths and hide my weaknesses."

INSPIRATION: "It's never what's obvious or on a runway."

PHILOSOPHY: "Get it together and get out the door. I am a single mom of a four-year-old so I don't have a lot of time to think about clothes. Fortunately, my daughter gives me a lot of opinions!"

erinn is an all-American beauty, full of energy and enthusiasm for life, work, and her daughter. Her clothes are classic but a little bit funky, well made, and practical. It's professional with a twist. "I don't have time to layer and overthink my clothes. I love one great, unexpected item that may take a bit more thought, and everything else falls into place," explains Erinn.

This stunning Empire-waist goddess dress was designed by Karen Foley. "I bought this dress for my boyfriend because it is a silhouette he really loves. The necklace is asymmetrical, "which is what I love about it," remarks Erinn. Her satin Manolo Blahniks were bought seven years ago, proving that great design never goes out of style.

SHAWN "This dress is by Mandalay. Everything they do is so intricate and well priced," says Shawn. The accessories are kept to a minimum since the jewelry is on the dress. It also has boning for shape, perfect for an upper-figured woman because it whittles the waist and accentuates the hips. Her hair is simple: it's just pulled back slightly so you can see her face and earrings. "So many women hide behind their hair and that's a shame because there are so many beautiful faces out there," says Shawn.

MERLE Merle wore this claret-colored dress by Dolce & Gabbana to a former boyfriend's formal Christmas party. "Everyone in Hollywood was going to be there and I wanted to knock them dead." This body-conscious dress did the trick, and it's perfect for Merle's hourglass curves. The beads are black jet. The Lizzie Scheck diamond necklace around her neck is her signature piece; Merle never takes it off.

CLAUDIA Tie-dye artist Carter Smith created Claudia's light-as-air silk chiffon ensemble, which glides over her body and gives her a regal appearance. It's perfect for black-tie events or romantic dinners. Claudia made the felted wool flower attached to her bracelet. The gorgeous tangle of necklaces includes strands she put together herself. as well as ropes made by her friend Hillary Bean. Claudia's Indian earrings are small emeralds set in 22-carat gold.

137

Sandy's Yves Saint-Laurent black silk dolman-style dress eases through the waist and tapers to a narrow point at the hem, disguising the waist and showing off her legs. Sandy draped the mink boa down her back for interest. Her vintage 18-carat gold cuffs with rubies and emeralds and the smoky topaz ring are by Tony Duquette. "I would wear this to any black-tie event. It's comfortable so I can enjoy the evening," says Sandy.

TAMARA Tamara loves staying home with her daughter, but her profession demands many evenings out. This Dolce & Gabbana dress meets the needs of any high-profile occasion. It's also an ideal silhouette for linear, hourglass, and upper-figured women. "I love its bohemian seventies feel. It's still sexy but glam," she says. The intricate necklace of gold and precious stones is Indian. "I find the most amazing jewelry in India," she says. Tamara also advises not to be afraid to mix jewelry with prints and patterns, as she does here. Note her simple ponytail. With an outfit like this, you don't need a fancy 'do!

NAME: Cheryl Tiegs

OCCUPATION: model and founder/ creator of the Ageless Woman skin care line

SHAPE: linear

STYLE: Classic Glamour Girl

INTENTION: "To make a glamorous style statement without exploding into a room or fading into the woodwork."

INSPIRATION: "I read fashion magazines, and certain friends of mine have great style."

PHILOSOPHY: "Be aware of what's current but always wear clothes that emphasize your best assets—never wear something simply because it's trendy."

MOTTO: "If you feel glamorous, you look glamorous!"

Cheryl Tiegs is one of the original supermodels, and her face has graced the covers of *Glamour, Elle, Vogue, Sports Illustrated* (three times!), and even *Time*. She's also a sophisticated businesswoman with an innate sense of style.

When she's really going out on the town, her look goes classic Hollywood. She rarely wears black because she loves the excitement of color. "For the most part I wear Randolph Duke for evening, and this goddess dress is a perfect example," she says.

The fitted jersey gown accentuates Cheryl's slender shape and creates curves. Elaborate accessories aren't necessary.

MARILYN This shirred chiffon dress is from one of my couture collections. Marilyn fell in love with it—I was a bit surprised actually, because I was not sure it was right for her. But seeing it on her made me change my mind. The bold, oversized houndstooth check is very modern, and the silhouette, with its deep V and soft gathers, is perfect for a linear woman because it emphasizes curves. "I love this dress because it's versatile. I wore it to a garden party and to Bouley for a dinner party," explains Marilyn. All she needs is a simple accessory such as this coral on a leather cord.

TOBI All work and no play is not what Tobi is about: she has made going out on the town an art, and she has the clothes to match. "I would wear this to a premiere, to the Ivy for dinner, or to any fall cocktail party in L.A.," she says. Her luxurious wrap skirt is made from heavy silk in a satin finish. The black halter top is backless and made from layers of tulle. This twosome works in unison to create a lean, curvy line. Tobi topped it off with a Gucci velvet motorcycle jacket and brown over-the-knee suede boots. Vintage black jet beads add even more glamour. "I would use the same mix of textures to design a house," she says.

CONSTANCE Constance even keeps her evening and black-tie looks streamlined and chic. "I bought this dress because it's so classic, and it's a great example of feminine French dressmaking."

This Hubert Givenchy–designed black silk dress can be accessorized in limitless ways. Here Constance paired it with white Manolo Blahniks and fishnets. "They take the prim and proper out of it. The fishnets are actually a sheer black stocking with a fishnet over them," says Constance. Rhinestone bracelets bring glamour to the ensemble. The blackened silver, filigree pearl, and rhinestone chandelier earrings are from eBay.

141

"**EVERY TIME**
a woman leaves off
SOMETHING,
she looks better;
BUT EVERY TIME
a man leaves off
SOMETHING,
he looks worse."

—Will Rogers,
cowboy, humorist, philosopher, and writer

finishing touches

ESSENTIAL ACCESSORIES

Everyone has to have a few well-chosen basic accessories to complement her versatile essential bottoms and tops. Necessities such as unfussy hoop earrings or a simple watch fill in the blanks, give polish to an outfit, and serve a practical purpose as well. More specific accessories such as a personality fringe belt or two-tone Louis-heeled shoes won't always show off a great black dress or a gabardine suit to its best advantage. In the main, you don't want background accessories to overpower your personality piece or draw attention away from a gorgeous neckline or your beautiful face! Essential accessories are successful when they accent and enhance you and your outfit without dominating it.

Essentials

De rigueur accessories are few but important. Some add a finishing touch to a thoughtfully constructed outfit. But you can also depend on these accessories to be "just enough" with a basic top and bottom when you want to go minimal or your intention is simply to dash off to a PTA meeting, or get to the wine shop for some champagne and back home to make dinner.

- **A simple watch**—in metal or with a leather strap.
- **A belt**—in a neutral color, probably black, tan, or brown with a simple metal buckle or one covered in the same leather.
- **Simple earrings**—gold or silver, hoops, studs, a colored stone in a simple setting, or whatever versatile pair suits you.
- **Handbag and tote**—dark leather for fall and winter daytime and a lighter color in straw, canvas, or leather for spring and summer. Small and medium totes are useful. Any bag that's too large looks like or maybe *is* a suitcase.
- **Shoes and boots**—you should have a flat shoe, a medium-heeled shoe, a high-heeled or evening shoe, an athletic shoe, and a sandal that fits your lifestyle. Most boots fall into the personality department, but if you live in a region where it gets cold and snowy, you'll need some essential waterproof ankle or knee-high boots that are versatile enough to take you to work or out to dinner. Think fleece- or fur-lined leather. Waterproof boots might even be necessary if you live in the country.
- **Sunglasses**—one all-purpose pair with UV protection for your eyes.
- **Hats**—a simple knit hat or a wool felt fedora is a must-have in northern climates for winter, and a good straw sun hat or canvas-brimmed cap is necessary to protect your face from the sun in summer, especially at the beach.

Handbags

A bag is an everyday accessory that few women can live without. Sometimes we do ourselves a disservice by carrying around too much junk in a bag that looks more like an old sack. Yet even when we pare down our needs, we still have so many things to carry around—cell phones, BlackBerries, planners, Palms, not to mention wallets, a little makeup and a comb or a brush, keys . . . Let's face it: there is no way to get around using some sort of bag.

What bag you buy depends on your budget. If you want one versatile bag, buy the best you can afford (see the shopping tips in chapter 11). Add fun, cheaper ones for changing moods. It's the most cost-effective way to go. You can spend $600 or more on a high-end designer beach bag—but is it necessary when you can find an inexpensive, perfectly cute, sturdy one while catalog shopping or at the mall? Add personal style to a plain canvas tote by tying a scarf around one of the handles for a little more color and flair, or pin an oversized brooch to it.

Whenever you buy a purse or a tote, remember to take into account your intentions (a day at the beach, commuting to work, dinner at a restaurant) so that you'll have enough room for what you need. Did you know that it's no longer necessary (or even preferable) to perfectly match your bag to your shoes? You do need to establish some connection between the two in terms of color tone and style. For example, team sleek modern black leather pumps and a vintage-style bag in the same leather. Or, black cowboy boots look great when you carry a tooled leather bag in light tan.

Really mismatched shoes and bags do not look balanced. A black patent-leather pump paired with a suede, fringed hobo bag is off the mark. Riding boots worn with a little satin clutch says bad planning more than anything. Better to pair the riding boots with a vintage leather handbag in a similar shade to achieve an interesting and pleasing paradox between rough-and-tumble outdoor living and tearoom propriety.

And if your bag is a personality piece because it's highly embellished or in a recognizable style (i.e., an Hermès Kelly bag) or a particularly vivid color (lime green, bright red), choose shoes and other accessories that fall into line behind it—items that are simple and noncompetitive.

Personal style will naturally guide your choice. If you're classic and tailored and work in an office, you may want to invest in one great bag to see you through weekdays in all seasons (think navy, black, brown, or beige) and then mix it up a bit on weekends with a cute little knapsack, a colorful cloth or straw bag, or a bright weatherproof tote. If you're a bohemian or a vintage-style woman, maybe your everyday bag is a patchwork shoulder bag, a designer handbag from the '50s, or a funky fashion bag in a hot color.

Have fun but don't forget that bags must also be functional. If you lead a very casual life, a structured bag may not work for you. Maybe you need something softer; a bag with a top opening that allows easy access is probably a good bet. If you are in a formal office every day, a bag with hard sides, a flap, and a snap closure looks neater and works better for your purpose—everything is safely contained for your commute or as you traverse urban streets.

If you are eclectic and want to change bags frequently depending on your outfits or the seasons, you may want three or four bags in different materials or colors (leather comes in every color under the sun these days—bright blue, hot pink, passionate purple, etc.). In this case, I would not splurge on designer bags. You can find serviceable fashion bags in every price range.

Evening Bags

Trends in evening bags don't change as often as other bag fashions, so special-occasion bags last for many seasons and see you through many events.

You can buy vintage if you want to use the bag as a personality piece with a simple evening gown. A 1920s beaded handbag or a 1950s velvet clutch with a rhinestone clasp looks great because it is unique. High-quality, beautifully constructed one-off or artist- or designer-made evening bags have a timeless appeal specifically because of their individuality. Keep in mind that if you have a very unique bag, its style is fixed. If it looks like a cabbage or a sleeping cat, it's going to look like that *forever*.

It's so easy to pick up a little satin clutch with a detachable strap these days, even at discount shoe and department stores. I like this idea, because it's so versatile. I belong to the "Morphing School of Fashion." I actually designed a simple black evening bag with a removable strap that you can replace with a chain or use as a clutch. From there, you can add your own little embellishments: tie, weave, or wrap a satin ribbon around your black bag's handle, or fix a flower or a rhinestone pin to the front of the bag. It's the perfect solution if you don't want to pay a fortune for more than one evening bag: a single bag becomes many.

Shoes and Boots

One pair of fabulous shoes can perk up last year's suit, jazz up a little black dress, and revitalize a simple turtleneck and trousers. Most of us are more willing to pay extra for an expensive pair of shoes by a favorite designer because it still costs less than buying an entire outfit from the same person. Some women inject their look with a jolt of excitement from budget-friendly fashion shoes and designer knockoffs. Beautiful shoes can be a wonderful diversion from perceived figure flaws, while still attracting the right kind of attention.

You're probably already familiar with which fabrics work for which season: open-toed shoes or strappy sandals with summertime looks; boots, closed-toe shoes, and leather shoes with buckles, visible contrasting stitching, or other ornaments for fall and winter simply because they look heavier. Aside from time of year, hem length is one of the most important factors in choosing a shoe. Knee-high boots are best with skirts. The higher the boot, the shorter the skirt can go. Ankle boots are great with pants and are very practical, too, in winter months.

Stacked heels and square-toed shoes look great with pants or longer full skirts. Narrow heels and rounded or pointier-toed shoes or boots are more feminine and look better with skirts and dress trousers. When wearing high heels with pants, ensure that the hems are long enough to cover most of the shoe, with about the bottom ¼ inch of the heel and the top of the front peeking out from under the hem. Pants that cover the entire shoe, with the hem almost touching the floor, are too long.

> "Adornment is never anything except a reflection of the heart."
>
> —Coco Chanel, clothing designer

shoe smarts

Shoes come in a variety of styles. Here's a primer on the most common styles.

Espadrille. A slip-on shoe of Spanish origin. The upper is usually made of a woven fabric such as canvas, and its flexible sole is covered with rope or grass.

Kitten heel. A pump with a 1- to 1½-inch heel that tapers sharply to a narrow base.

Mule. A closed-toe shoe of any heel height with no back. Also known as a slip-on shoe.

Platform. A shoe, boot, or sandal with thick, high soles, often made of cork, plastic, rubber, or wood (wooden platform shoes are known as clogs).

Pump. A shoe whose vamp and sides are cut close to the toe box.

Spectator pump. A medium-heeled pump with contrasting colors on the toe and the heel.

Stacked-heel shoe. A shoe with a 1½- to 3½-inch heel that has horizontal lines, indicating that it is made up of stacked layers of leather.

Stiletto. A pump defined by a high heel that is pointy, thin, and at least 3 inches high.

Wedge. A shoe typically with a mid- to high heel, and where the heel and the sole form a solid block, with no gap under the instep.

style diary

The Old Switcheroo

Get together with two of your best girlfriends and bring all the accessories you have that are in good condition and that you haven't worn in a while. Tell everyone to wear her most basic outfit (white blouse and black pants, navy turtleneck and camel pencil skirt). Spread out everything on the floor and start exchanging. Try different shoes, bags, scarves, and jewelry against the backdrop of your classic outfits. See how many different looks you can create with accessories alone. Two things happen: you learn a lot about the power of accessories and you refresh what you have (without spending a dime). Take chances and shake up things when you accessorize!

Stiletto heels (3 inches or higher) are fabulous if you know how to walk in them. Wobbling down the street isn't graceful and can be dangerous. You have to practice walking in stilettos, but if you do so and still can't manage it, you may want to go a little lower with a 2-inch heel (not everyone can or should wear stilettos). If you are short and want to elongate your look, slender heels or Louis heels afford a similar effect to high heels, and they are often more sculpted or refined than sky-high stilettos.

Shorter women may want to avoid shoes with horizontal stripe details, such as straps. They are better for taller girls with thin ankles. If you are tall and don't want to tower over everyone, a little 1½-inch heel elongates the leg in a sexy way. In general, any heel that gives you a little lift is going to slim and lengthen your frame and add a nice curve to your calf.

If you are middle figured, avoid very tall, slim heels, which leave you literally and visually teetering off balance. The middle-figured woman is better off with a wider or shorter heel or a narrow rounded-toe flat. The linear-figured woman can go with a shoe with some embellishment or contrast for balance. The hourglass woman can wear almost any shoe or boot that suits her size and height. If you're a slim upper-figured woman, you can wear any style of shoe or boot, as can the lower-figured woman. If, however, you're lower or upper figured but larger, you may want to avoid very delicate shoes. Any woman can wear any style of heel as long as her ankles are small and her calves shapely and long. As with all elements of your outfit, the choice comes down to balance and proportion. How do the shoes look with what you are wearing?

Belts

Belts are often overlooked as an accessory. And they are not just for your waist anymore! Belts can sit lower than your waist and, depending on your figure, can even encircle your hips. They can go through the loops of jeans or pants, or buckle neatly over a sweater that just hits your hips. You can even belt a dress.

Almost everyone can wear a belt if it is placed properly on the torso. A belt cinched too tightly on the waist accentuates not only your middle but also your hips and bust, so be careful. Normally, a good guideline to follow for a belt worn on the waist is that it fits when it comfortably buckles on the third hole. If you can go farther than that, the belt is too large. Anything less, such as the first hole, and you probably want to go one size up.

It's best for middle-figured or very short-waisted women to avoid anything that circles or emphasizes the waist, particularly anything very narrow or delicate. Other accessories will probably suit better. Linear-figured women benefit from a wider waist or hip belt, because it's an easy way to create a curve and break up the straight vertical lines. Consider choosing a belt in a contrasting color to the outfit, or even a tonal color in a shade lighter or darker. Decorative stitching, fancy buckles, or other embellishments are good options for linear-figured women. Scarves as tie belts flatter. Linear women should avoid very narrow belts.

Hourglass women can wear belts of any width. Decorative buckles, which draw even more attention to the middle, are an option, too. But be careful: in a tightly drawn belt, the hourglass woman may look like a sausage tied in the middle, not to mention that these belts are uncomfortable to wear for any period of time.

Wide, hip-style belts or those that rest just below the waistline help the upper-figured woman, as they elongate the torso. Wear them slightly loose and avoid oversized buckles, which shorten the waist and emphasize the bust.

Lower-figured women can use the same trick as upper-figured women, with a soft, medium-width belt worn slightly lower in the front than in the back. A belt buckled at the waist emphasizes the behind.

Jewelry

Jewelry is inherently personal. It is such a beautiful adornment that I think women can look a little plain without any. And face it, when you put on great jewelry, it makes you feel important, radiant, and rich.

I like jewelry that says something—give me one big great ring. A lot of stylish women seem to wear very personal pieces of jewelry that convey a message, and they may even mix it with more classic pieces. For example, an African cuff, Bakelite pins, and vintage cameos all make appearances on stylish women's outfits as essentials, right alongside the button earrings or the metal watch.

ring around the collar

No matter what your Shape of Style, if you have a short or a thick neck, avoid chokers or big beads that encircle and emphasize it!

The biggest myth by far about jewelry is that certain things are inappropriate. Pearls worn with a twinset, while pretty, is safe and predictable. Pearls with a denim jacket, on the other hand, might be just what the outfit needs to throw the casual look off in a very pretty way. Mixing dressy or traditional jewelry with informal garments is exciting. And jewelry is unpredictable: a cameo may look antiquated on an older woman, but when a younger woman mixes it with denim and lace, it takes on a whole new look and life. The mature woman may appear more up to date with a stark modern piece, especially when fixed to something really classic, such as a Chanel-style suit.

There are a few guidelines when it comes to jewelry. In general, if you are going to mix different styles of jewelry, keep them in the same metal. If the forms are *similar*—modern and modern, vintage with vintage, and so on—yellow gold and silver blend nicely. You can mix with abandon if they are in the same metal tones. Modern pieces in yellow gold work with gold vintage; Edwardian-age platinum items work with 1960s silver retro jewelry.

I really like silver because it draws a lot of light. My mother used to wear all gold jewelry all the time when she was younger; now she wears silver, which looks great because it's fresh and young. In general, silver compliments cool skin and eye tones; gold compliments warm tones.

Matching skin tone to jewelry isn't absolutely necessary. Skin tone

"I've never thought of my jewelry as trophies. I'm here to take care of it and to love it."

—Elizabeth Taylor, actress

changes with the seasons, and the contrast of metals with skin tone can serve a fashion purpose; everyone's skin tone warms up a bit in the summer, but silver cools it down. Gold's warmth and earthiness add richness, expecially in the winter, when most of us feel a little pale. Olive skin looks good against the cool contrast of silver or nickel. Darkly tanned skin can look somewhat bland when paired with gold. And pale skin with cool silver isn't always a great combination.

I also don't like it when the jewelry wears you. When you put on jewelry and it's the only thing you see, consider taking some or all of it off. Generally, the simpler the outfit, the more complex, elaborate, and specific the jewelry can be.

Scarves, Wraps, and Shawls

Scarves and wraps can add a shot of color around your face and break up the boring lines of a monochromatic dress or coat. Wraps and shawls are practical. They keep you warm on chilly evenings, and a beautiful pashmina can take the place of an expensive and most likely rarely used evening coat for formal nights.

No matter what kind of scarf you use, keep your shape in mind. Middle-figured women should avoid tying scarves at the neck, which draws the eye to the bust. A shawl wrapped around the shoulders works better. Linear women benefit by using a large scarf, folded into a triangle, and tied at the waist. The simple oblong pull through also flatters and breaks up the straight lines. Hourglass women can experiment with all sorts of scarf tricks. Upper-figured women are better off with wraps and scarves used as belts or hip wraps or head coverings. Lower-figured women really benefit by any scarf style used at the neck or around the shoulders.

A scarf doesn't have to go around your neck. It can be used as a belt—a silk twill scarf makes a great belt with jeans, for example. It can be tied around a purse or a tote for a little color and flair. It can be wrapped around your head as a turban or a simple kerchief (an iconic Jackie O look when paired with dark sunglasses). You can wrap a scarf into a bandeau or a halter top, too. A large sarong can even be worn as a halter dress, a strapless dress, or a wrap skirt! I once made an evening gown out of a length of fabric—basically a really big scarf—and secured it with a big brooch.

Fabric squares from 36 to 45 inches (standard yardage widths) make great wrap skirts; oblongs 36 to 45 inches by 54 to 72 inches make great bandeaus or halter tops. Squares of 54 or 60 inches (also standard yardage widths) make great wrap skirts and dresses. Next time you are in a fabric store, check out the silky yardage—it could be your next no-sew date dress!

Glasses and Sunglasses

Some of you need glasses out of necessity, but you can still make a fashion statement with them. And even those of you who don't need glasses to see or read *do* need sunglasses to protect your eyes and create an aura of mystery!

Look for eyeglasses that contrast with and complement your skin tone and eye color. Darker-colored glasses flatter pale skin, and darker skin tones look best with lighter-colored glasses. With sunglasses, you can play it fast and loose—they're worn outside, so you have a lot of leeway to play. (*Please* take your sunglasses off when you are indoors!)

Frames come in myriad shapes and sizes, so try them on before you make your choice. Wide oval or rectangular shapes with slight cat's-eye curves flatter round faces. Look for frames that are wider than they are tall. Strong vertical frames flatter long faces—anything that has a horizontal shape elongates the face further. They also look nice on square faces. Butterfly frames, rounded frames, and frameless glasses look pretty on heart-shaped faces.

style diary

It's in the Bag!

Be a paper bag princess again, just like in chapter 2, but this time with your clothes *on*. Put your bag mask back on when you have completed your outfit and have added your essential accessories, but *before* you do your hair and makeup. Now look in the mirror. Who's that girl in the mirror—is she hot? What do you think of her? Is her look harmonious? Are you feeling it? Is she pulled together? If not, what can she change about her outfit to make it better? Take something off? Maybe add something? The paper bag trick allows you to assess your outfit in the most objective way possible, short of having a friend or a professional with you. Try it—you won't believe how well it works to take the emotional aspect out of evaluating your look.

"Personality is the glitter that sends your little gleam across the footlights and the orchestra pit into that big black space where the audience is."

—Mae West, actress

the all-important personality piece

I've mentioned "personality pieces" a few times in this book, but up until now I haven't gone into depth on what they are. Your personality pieces are *the* most Important elements of your wardrobe. They define your mood, cause a bit of a stir, and sometimes make a little trouble (of the best kind, of course). They are your ensemble's exclamation point. Personality pieces elevate your essential silhouettes into highly individual outfits. • Don't confuse the personality piece with your signature (if you happen to have one). Your ubiquitous bob or ever-present pearls are not necessarily the ingredients that give your outfit personality. A signature is consistent; a personality piece changes from outfit to outfit, mood to mood, intention to intention.

Personality pieces are garments, accessories, or even a hairstyle that has *specificity.* In other words, their characteristics or details are the opposite of generic. The list of possibilities is endless: suede mules with a kitten heel, handmade cowboy boots with metal stud detailing, a vegetable-dyed Indian poncho or a hand-loomed paisley wrap from Morocco, an animal-print African tunic, a Tyrolean velvet-trimmed jacket, a bold but minimalist silver necklace, an armful of Bakelite bangle bracelets, a vintage Pucci scarf, or even a French braid. Any of these would be your outfit's personality piece. Even the elaborate lace trim on your camisole peeking out of your power suit can play the personality role. It's subtle in this instance, but it's still the *focus* or *spice* of your outfit.

The essential black pants or basic sweater becomes something special with the help of a personality piece. That doesn't mean everything you wear around the personality piece must be bare-bones basic—a brightly colored shift or wrap dress gets added excitement with a large flower pin, for example. Or a pink tweed jacket and jeans can be revved up with three or four cross pendants. And a personality piece does not necessarily have to make a huge statement. It's not only about glitz and sparkle. The personality piece is effective even when subtle. Spare, understated separates make powerful personality pieces: think about a great butter-suede jacket or a finely knit cashmere shawl; they say luxury and opulence. The message may be restrained, but it's still strong.

Before you add personality pieces to your wardrobe, take some time to assess what you already have. Make it fun. Take an hour for

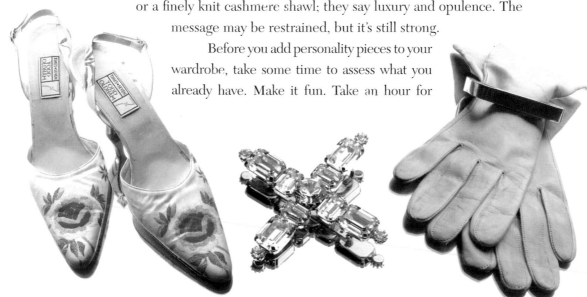

yourself, pull out your least generic clothes, dust off every accessory, and assess what you have. Which items are specific enough to function as personality pieces? How many different ways can you use them? You may be surprised to find your personality shoe or jacket gives an old standby outfit a totally new look and personality! For example, your personality-piece high-heeled shoes look great with a chiffon dress—but they also add supercharged character to jeans and a little silk top. Or a chunky beaded bracelet might look perfect with simple navy trousers and a white T—turning up the volume on what is already a pretty and classic outfit. That Edwardian cameo you haven't worn in *years* may be just the contradictory element your worn leather bomber jacket needs. A fantastic outsized midcentury modern bag you scored at a flea market may make a perfect beach tote. Or your beach tote may make the perfect summer work tote! Use an accessory meant for one purpose in another way, and it becomes brand-new.

There is a kind of science to selecting personality pieces. You may feel a little fear in the beginning, but once you get the hang of it, it's your chance to break your own rules. For beginners, the overwhelming part is delineating the personality piece for a particular outfit. Playing around with what you have is the best way to learn how to do that.

"Bravery never goes out of fashion."

—William Thackeray, *novelist*

In general, when selecting personality pieces to suit your shape, keep in mind the guidelines in chapter 3. As long as you stay within your silhouettes, tremendous freedom of choice is yours. Make sure the personality piece accentuates or plays up your assets and helps distract from features you want to minimize.

When you first begin consciously selecting personality pieces, it is less overwhelming, not to mention easier, if you stick to one per outfit. It won't take long for you to be an expert and you'll know how to layer four personality pieces in one outfit with success. It takes practice to know when and how to blend the high with the low, the prints with the patterns, the beads with the bangles, and so on. To be sure your look comes together beautifully and effortlessly in a cohesive picture, refresh yourself on the "Pulling It Together" section in chapter 4.

personality

shape of style:

These Shape of Style reminders will help you select that "just right" personality piece.

LINEAR FIGURED

For garments, a personality dress, top, jacket, pants, or skirt are all excellent possibilities, but avoid vertical prints and lines. Bold prints and colors that pop are fine. Accessories such as square, oval, or round handbags and totes, belts, and sashes flatter, as do shawls and boots. Chunky jewelry, such as wide bracelets, large bead necklaces, large amulets on long chains or cords, and oversized rings, are great choices.

THE HOURGLASS

Almost any kind of personality piece suits, including boldly printed dresses and decorative belts, bold necklaces, fancy shoes and boots, and elaborate handbags.

pieces

MIDDLE FIGURED

For clothing, consider a jacket in your Shape of Style Silhouette. Think twice about a personality-piece dress or pants—better to make these essential elements of your outfit. Focus on accessories that accentuate the face, such as beautiful scarves, ornamental earrings, hair ornaments, and upswept hairdos. Personality shoes and bags also balance the middle-figured woman. Avoid fancy belts, heavy bangles, and anything else that accentuates the waist.

LOWER FIGURED

Bring your personality-piece clothing to your upper half in the form of snazzy jackets, detailed blouses, blazers made from woven or other interestingly textured fabrics, decorative sweaters, and one-of-a-kind shirts. For accessories, consider shoes, boots, and bags. Go all out with jewelry, especially earrings, chokers (if you have a long, slender neck), amulets, and multiple strands of long beads. Shawls, scarves, and wraps are excellent options. Think twice about lots of bracelets and large rings.

UPPER FIGURED

For clothing, choose personality-piece pants and skirts—and keep the top simple. For example, try a glittery skirt instead of a sequined jacket for dressy evenings. Neck scarves and wraps in solid or muted prints are accessory options. Long beaded necklaces and chains create a long line and bring the eye down to your lower half. Consider adding unusual shoes, boots, bags, and totes to your outfits. Think twice about chunky chokers, short necklaces, and wide belts.

Don't worry if your choices don't always succeed with flying colors; sometimes they just won't. One evening, my personality piece (yes, men should have them, too!) was a gauze shirt with a giant pink-and-green floral print. The jeans I had on were almost too Warren-Beatty-in-*Shampoo* obvious. That's why it didn't work—maybe green khaki pants would have worked better. I had gone to a restaurant and I felt self-conscious that people were looking at the outfit; that was not my intention. I wanted them to look at me *in* the outfit.

The outfit was wearing me, if you know what I mean. Before you venture out, ask yourself, especially regarding a theatrical personality piece, if you want to be the star or if you want the clothes to take the lead role. How do you want to be perceived? Have you accomplished your intention? If not, go back to the closet and try again.

To make it even easier to choose your personality pieces, we'll go category by category, starting with individual clothing items as personality pieces, then accessories—belts, shoes, bags, scarves, and jewelry.

Through it all, always take the liberty to try new things and unusual combinations. You'll gain confidence this way, and practice makes perfect. The feeling that the right personality pieces evoke is truly mind-altering. Forget about the antidepressant; get the pink sweater out if you're feeling blue! There's a whole world of tasty things to experience—don't miss out.

Where's the Personality in Your Closet?

Clothing

Standout items like a patchwork skirt, a buffalo plaid jacket, or gold satin pants are *not* neutral. They have a life of their own, a point of view. Some extraordinary items never really go out of fashion, and you can wear them for as long as you love them. It's about the incredible 1980s American designer's bejeweled jacket or a Japanese kimono or an Indian sari or a mint-condition vintage Pucci dress. You don't throw out stuff like that. Maybe you don't wear it for a year. Then after a hiatus, all of a sudden it looks fresh again. Such garments are really works of art. I don't think you need too many of these—it's up to your personal preference. How do you tell which items are classics in the making, and which will become dated? Read on. . . .

Wearing highly individual clothes successfully depends on what you pair with them. Up-to-date essentials (the white shirt, the boot-cut black pant, the slim V-neck T) act as a neutral backdrop for one-of-a-kind garments. Investing in personality clothes makes sense if you have the basics to back them up. For example, say you buy a pricy beaded paisley skirt because you love it and it happens to be the right silhouette for your shape. There's no question something that specific would be a personality piece—it's certainly not essential.

But specific clothing doesn't have to be limited to certain uses or circumstances. No matter how particular a garment is, it could still be cost-effective if it is versatile. The beaded paisley skirt is dressy with stilettos and a sheer chiffon blouse. But the same skirt looks funky enough for a weekend brunch when worn with a cotton ribbed turtleneck and riding boots. When you're thinking about buying a personality garment, ask yourself how many ways you can wear it: Can you really put it to work? Or must it be relegated to one-occasion-only dressing? Can the satin pants be easily dressed up or down according to your intention? Does the jersey top look great with

what's bad

The best way to distinguish between great clothes and mediocre ones is to look at a lot of clothes. Seriously. With practice you can discern good design from bad ideas, quality manufacturing (more on that in chapter 11) from poor workmanship. Trust your eye—you can tell first-rate from inferior if you just spend time looking. If you are really interested in expanding your knowledge of style, go to a fashion retrospective at a museum or read any one of dozens of good books about fashion history and style makers.

jeans, shorts, a skirt and a jacket, velvet pants, or a ballgown-style skirt? If the answer is yes and you love it, it's a good piece to have in your closet.

Understated personality pieces can be quite effective, too. If you are going on a job interview and it's a fairly conventional office, your intention is to impress *and* reassure. In that case, a subtle jacket or top might be the personality piece. Interviews happen face-to-face, so the personality should

Decorate It!

Express your personality and stretch your creativity by embellishing your clothes. The simple application of cording, ribbon trim, or beading gives you a "new" garment. All you need is the trim and some fabric glue (available at craft and sewing stores), the straight-stitch setting on a sewing machine, or a needle and thread.

If you are afraid that anything you do will look homemade in a bad way, or if you think it's going to look too "crafty" or cutesy, please reconsider. Some of the most sophisticated women I know add embellishment to their clothes. I have a friend in L.A. who is very East Coast chic. She bought beaded diamond trim and had a tailor sew it to a jacket. Underneath the jacket she wore a vintage lace blouse. Wow. I wager that your local dry cleaner has a tailor available to do such simple sewing jobs for very little money. The trick is choosing just the right extras.

Here are just a few suggestions:

- Add ribbon trim to the placket of a cardigan for a designer look.
- Glue beading to the bottom of your jeans or glue a long line of beaded fringe to the outer seam.
- Attach a fabric cuff to a denim jacket.
- Trim the hem of a simple black dress with decorative fringe.
- Stitch three rows of grosgrain ribbon onto the bottom of an A-line skirt.
- Fasten glass-bead fringe to the hem of a skirt, pants, or even shorts.
- Cover spaghetti straps on a tank with a line of beads, sequins, or pearls.
- Sew individual Venetian beads onto the bodice of a sheer top.
- Swathe the lapel of a blazer with lots of silk flowers, so it's totally encrusted.
- Use a fabric paint marker and make dots or stripes on a cotton shirt cuff and collar.
- Take a bleach pen to your jeans using a damask-pattern stencil; you can do the same on jeans with a stencil roller and paint.

be on your top half and help project your strength, commitment, and intelligence—but without being too distracting. Maybe it's a very tailored jacket with beautiful dressmaker details. Or it's a strong color that suggests you are not like everyone else but can still fit into the corporate culture. If you are going on a job interview at a more casual office, or a creative shop, maybe you go out on a ledge a little more. But since interviews are fairly intimate, no matter what the size or the culture of the office, it's a good idea to keep the personality around or near your face and shoulders.

All women, even upper-figured ladies, can use strong color near their faces in a simple T or one-button tailored blazer, or through accessories such as a silk scarf. All imply self-possessed confidence. Sometimes all the personality your outfit needs is a shot of bold color. It can pop your whole look. For instance, a hot pink cashmere sweater worn with an otherwise neutral outfit will create a stir, both psychologically and visually. Perhaps it's just the punch you need on that interview to keep your energy level up (as if your nerves don't!).

Accessories

Shoes adorned with feathers, bags embroidered with beads and dripping with fringe, belts that close with buttons—accessories are absolutely kaleidoscopic today. You can truly rely on these whimsical pieces to add personality and color to a basic outfit. Classic combinations like the navy top and pants or the beige skirt and white blouse are lifted by a bit of "bling" on the edges of your outfit.

All the essentials—the great black dress, the skirt suit, the black pants and white shirt—are endlessly tranformed depending on the accents around them. A lot of times the accessory personality piece is your favorite item of the moment—your much-loved crocodile-embossed bag or little multicolored knit cloche hat, for example. The accessory sets the tone of the outfit. For example, say we put a woman in a black shift, a hair band, and flats. She looks preppy. Take off the shoes and the hair band and put her in a leather choker and black leather stilettos with chain detail, and she looks sexy and slightly dangerous. That's the power of personality accessories.

Play with personality accessories! Learn what you like and what looks fabulous on you. If you are attracted to a madras plaid scarf or a hippie belt, wear it and feel good when you put it on. You'll become more adept at making distinctions as time goes on. After a while you will start to notice that you need more than one cross around your neck with a certain silhouette, or you'll recognize the beaded cross is not right when you're wearing something tailored, but the sleek silver cross is just the thing.

Jewelry

Jewelry is the ultimate personality piece by virtue of its sheer range of styles, colors, materials, and price points. Beautiful jewelry is accessible to all. It's versatile and transformative. A long, modern silver pendant serves as the calm Zenlike centerpiece of a monochromatic cream-and-beige or black outfit. A pile of multicolored Moroccan beads around the neck brings the exotic to a simple shift. A polished quartz pendant adds sophistication to a turtleneck and jeans. Turquoise rings and bracelets give you the air of a collector—even if you bought them simply because you *love* the way they look.

Great jeans, a white shirt, and a cardigan go down a whole different road when complemented by several strands of Venetian glass beads mixed with golden chains so long they reach your belt. Keep the outfit the same: substituting Native American jewelry takes you to a whole other place, and sleek sculptural sterling silver Elsa Peretti jewelry brings you somewhere else again. All destinations say Important. With jewelry as your personality piece, do you really need anything *other than* the jeans, shirt, and sweater? An exaggeration, perhaps, but you see my point.

> ""Life is serious, but art is fun.""
>
> —John Irving, novelist

Don't be afraid to play with size and scale. For dramatic effect, try wearing a large-scale necklace with tiny earrings. Think about using personality jewelry in unconventional ways. For evening, put brooches in creative places: the placement *and* the pin become your outfit's personality. For example, if you are wearing a low-backed dress, placing a brooch on the back of the dress is provocative. If the dress has a side slit, place a pin where the opening starts. Use oversized pins as belt buckles or place matching pins on the vamp or top of shoes.

Play around with abundance. Multiples can be smashing. You *almost* can't have too much repetition when it comes to jewelry. How about two or three watches on your wrist? Rings on every finger? Try three pendants instead of one. The only caution? Stick with one kind of item at a time: if you pile jewelry on your wrists, fingers, neck, *and* jacket lapel, you'll end up looking like a walking jewelry store (and forget about getting past airport security!).

Dressing on the Edge

By now, you've probably started taking some risks. Keep it up! Personal style, after all, is not just about getting dressed; it's about theater and communication—and your personality piece speaks the loudest. That doesn't mean you should dye your hair pink or buy thigh-high fake leopard-skin boots. Not yet, anyway. . . .

This is where you have to run to your husband's or son's or girl-friend's closet to see how very contrary clothing feels. This is the point at which you challenge your comfort level—maybe nothing you try on ends up being you. The point is, we don't play enough. You have to take the time and let your reaction be your guide—because you know when you don't feel right and you know when you are happy as a lark.

style diary

Throw a T-shirt Party

Buy a bunch of inexpensive white T-shirts, gather a few close girlfriends, and assemble scissors, fabric markers, dye for tie-dying, fabric glue, needles and silk embroidery floss, grosgrain ribbon, buttons, fabric scraps, jewelry odds and ends—anything you can think of that can be attached, sewed on, or glued to fabric. And then go crazy—what can you come up with? Get your creative juices flowing—and have fun!

MERLE Merle loves her linen-and-cotton-blend Rochas jacket with tulle detailing. "I think tulle is my favorite thing in the world; it must come from a weird, twisted ballerina fantasy," she says.

CLAUDIA "Anything tie-dyed would be my personality piece," says Claudia. "Between my kids, my husband, and myself, we have hundreds of tie-dyed T-shirts!"

MARILYN "I wanted something unusual and thought about hand painting," explains Marilyn, "and Jeffrey was excited about it." She first considered a graffiti print, but Jeffrey Fulvimar, the illustrator, steered her toward something more graphic, and painted the elaborate swirls down just one leg.

ERINN A major piece of clothing can be a personality piece, as is the case with this one-of-a-kind dress made from vintage fabrics. "It's casual and elegant. I have worn it to a beach party in Big Sur and out to dinner in New York," says Erinn.

"The excitement of beauty lies in the ability to look different."

—Kevyn Aucoin, makeup artist

the grand finale

HAIR AND MAKEUP

Hair and makeup are the icing on the
cake of personal style. What's most important? Not getting stuck in a rut. We have all
seen women who wear the same haircut
and makeup for years, even decades.
They stopped playing around with
new looks when they graduated
from high school or college.
That doesn't have to be you.
You can experiment; you can
change your look constantly
or seasonally, if you want. In
fact, if you haven't changed your
hair and makeup in a year or more,
it's time to reevaluate!   •   I look at hair
and makeup from a fashion point of view.
That means I'm less technically oriented, and I
see your haircut or makeup as an accessory that
offers added ways to express your personal style.

Seek counsel from professionals whenever you make changes or if you feel less than confident about your skills with a blow dryer or a blush brush. Makeup that's applied incorrectly draws attention away from your best features and plays up aspects you'd rather not advertise. A great haircut or hairstyle can change your world, but bad ones can ruin it (at least for a while!). Invest in a trip to a good salon and a lesson from a makeup artist. All cities and large towns have skilled experts—and they don't necessarily cost a fortune. In fact, you can save yourself a lot of money in the long run if you invest in a few essentials you like and need, rather than needlessly buying lots of stuff you're not really happy with.

Hair Fair!

The Bad Hair Day is not a joke. Haven't you noticed that when you feel good about your hair, everything else seems to fall into place? But when our hair misbehaves, every aspect of our day feels off kilter. The best solution to keeping bad hair days at bay is to maintain your mane in top condition, find a cut that suits your face and lifestyle, and avoid a style rut at all costs. People don't experiment enough with hair. It's another way of shifting your frame of mind. If you're a blonde, do you feel sexier when you go a few shades darker? If you wear your hair long and down, do you become more authoritative when you put it up? Or, if your hair is short and controlled, do you feel liberated when you don't style it so precisely?

By all means, put a hair change on your calendar; schedule it just as you would a business meeting! "In two months, or over the summer, I am going to get a new look." Give yourself something to look forward to even if it is simply parting your hair on the opposite side, adding bangs, or growing out bangs. Sticking to the same hairstyle gets boring. It's like looking at the same picture all the time. Change is rejuvenating and often a revelation.

Hair is like a costume, so consider getting a haircut with versatility for different events and intentions. That might mean hair just long enough to be altered easily from time to time. Your hair does not have to be terribly long for you to put it up, slick it back, or wear it full. If you pull your hair back in a ponytail, it's young and casual. When you pull it up and off your face and secure it with a rhinestone clasp, it's formal. You can do the sexy bed head mussy thing with longer or shorter hair, especially when it is layered. Highly architectural cuts are more difficult to manipulate because their personality comes from their structure. But a layered cut can be maneuvered around and blown dry to look structured or not.

How do you begin finding a new style? Here, you need input from others. First, get opinions on your current style. People won't lie if you ask sincerely, "Tell me the truth, what do you think? I really want to know." Ask five people individually and notice any common denominators in their responses. Select a coworker, a friend, a relative, an acquaintance, and a stranger. (Women never mind being asked their opinion by another woman in a store and they often give you the most honest answer.) If everyone says, "Your 1980s wings are a little dated," it's time for them to go. If you hear, "Something off your face would be very nice," try pulling your hair back. This is just the beginning.

Next, get tear sheets together by pulling examples from magazines. But be realistic! Look for styles on women who have hair that seems similar to yours in texture—realize that if you have fine hair, your results will differ from

longing for long

Women have a tendency to get addicted to what I call The Long of It All because they feel sexy with long hair. You can wear long hair at any age. I don't know of any law that says you have to chop off your hair when you're forty or fifty or sixty. *But*, and this is a big but, long hair has to be in good condition. That means trimmed and neat. Bad long hair is really bad. It won't do you any favors if it's too long and dry and not smooth looking. Long hair demands to be cared for: broken hair is not sexy. You are better off getting an inch taken off regularly (every few weeks) to freshen it and clean up the ends. And you have to ask yourself if you have the time to take care of your long hair. Can you get it trimmed on a regular basis? Are you able to keep it in shiny, healthy condition? Are you *always* willing to take the time to make it look its best? Do you have enough resources to invest in maintaining your long hair?

to curl or
not to curl

You can now go curly or straight depending on your preference. Technology and new products let you change whatever you have—or don't have. Try it both ways. What's your intention? Do you feel girly and flirty in curly hair? Or do you feel sexy and sophisticated when you go straight? Think about it!

yours in texture—realize that if you have fine hair, your results will differ from the images of women with curly or coarse hair. What looks do you gravitate toward? The litmus test is your first response. It's always right. If you are picking photos of women with pulled-back hair, or long wavy hair, that thread helps you determine what you want when discussing a cut with your hairstylist.

Finally, never feel you must cut your hair a certain way just because of a trend. Get a cut that does *your* hair, face, and lifestyle justice! I disagree with the idea that if a bob is in style, you should get one. You'll have to maintain whatever cut you get. How much time do you have to devote to styling and general maintenance? If a particular cut requires blow-drying each morning to look its best, that cut may not be for you.

Let your hairstylist help you decide what cut flatters your face. He or she has assessed hundreds of faces and hair types—take advantage of his or her knowledge.

Color Time

Hair color is a big issue, loaded with danger. The proclivity to color your hair is very strong for many of you, I know. A lot of you want to enhance what nature gave you or just mix it up a bit with a new color. Your sense of urgency, or maybe boredom, fuels the rush to the drugstore for the "solution in a box," and the ensuing mistakes and regrets make the outcome worse. Beware of the kits in the grocery store! Take it from me: paying for corrective color treatments in a salon because of an at-home color mishap is far more expensive than having a professional tint your hair from the get-go.

If you want great color and highlights, go to a colorist you trust! It's better to invest the time and the money and go to a professional who knows how to blend tints for your specific hair and coloring.

A professional colorist helps you achieve a flattering color that looks real. Look at your natural shade as a clue to what direction to take. Don't assume you must go lighter. If you try a shade too drastically different from what nature has given you, your eye and skin color look off balance and you have to wear a great deal of makeup to compensate for the difference. Do you have time for all that?

I also warn against what I call the Blonding of America. Too much! We have a tendency to lighten hair as we age because it's perceived as youthful. Caution! You can get to the point of being a "beige lady," and the really light colors end up working against you. Or worse, you can lighten your hair so much it just ends up looking dry and white and ratty. You have to see hair color in the context of your overall coloring. It's not for me to say, "Don't have your hair highlighted," but a little goes a long way. Start with less and if you want more, go back to the salon for it.

The best way to find the right hair color is to take inspiration from a color that already exists in your hair and play that up with subtle highlights. If you are a brunette with some auburn, try copper or red highlights. If you are a medium blonde with dark blond mixed in, add lighter blond highlights mixed with light brown lowlights for added dimension. If you have very dark brown hair, maybe you can try going black or a really deep mahogany. And nonpermanent washes in more natural tones provide a chance to try on some different colors before you commit to a permanent situation.

style diary

Parting Ways

Try parting your hair in different ways—I do this when I am bored on Sunday night. It makes me laugh, but sometimes I find a different part really works! Parting your hair on a different side also makes your hair appear thicker. Sunday night will never be the same.

Makeup Simplified

Intention plays a crucial role in what makeup you wear and how you apply it. Are you going for a clean and simple look, a fashion look, a sexy look, or a business look? First you have to decide if you are a makeup type or an on-the-go, less-makeup type. In my experience, a light makeup person is not going to become a "heavy user" all of a sudden. That is especially true if you are in the thirty to fifty age group. It's unrealistic to think you are going to start wearing full-face makeup every day. Your habits, routine, and lifestyle determine how much makeup you use. So first and foremost you have to be true to yourself.

Next, you have to find the right foundation. Most women over age thirty need a good foundation, even if it is a very sheer one. Getting it right from a color standpoint means understanding your skin tone. Ruddy and pink complexions need yellow-based foundation for balance. If the skin is more yellow, makeup with a pink base neutralizes the complexion. Before you buy, make sure to test a sample on your jawline. When you smooth the sample on your skin, it should disappear but still offer sheer coverage.

clean up your act!

Go through your makeup bag and get rid of anything you haven't worn in six months. Replace mascaras and lipsticks that are more than three months old. Keep brushes and other implements clean, and don't share makeup with friends!

After you've settled on a foundation, begin to play with your lips and eyes. I recommend downplaying one and emphasizing the other. For example, if you want rich, red lips, ease up on the eye shadow. A little mascara and liner may be enough. If you want smoky eyes, a sheer gloss is all your lips really need. Accentuating lips and eyes at the same time results in a heavy and artificial look.

The role of everyday makeup is to enhance what you have and play up your best features. Keep it real for daytime: a little light foundation to even out skin tone and cover imperfections, some blush on the apples of your cheeks, a sweep of mascara, and a pinch of lip gloss can see you through a lot!

Night Lights

There are times when you want to wear special makeup for evening or for seduction. Fashion makeup is more obvious and playful than what you put on every day. It's deliberate. Add some glitter on your cheeks or collarbone, draw a line of smoldering eyeliner on your lids, or put on some sultry shine with dimensional lip gloss as a way of playing up your features. See what you think—if you feel ridiculous with too much on, you are not going to feel sexy!

Individual eyelashes (applied by a pro only) are fabulous for your personal red-carpet moments. Feathering a standard row of them with cuticle scissors before you glue them onto your lash line has a similar effect, but you are really better off having them applied individually. It's an incredible look. Instant face-lift!

If you are going out straight after work, change one thing about your makeup and you'll feel more glam. Just the act of adding more lipstick or eyeliner makes you feel like you are pampering yourself. That's part of the shift from work to play. A little extra emphasis on either the lips or the eyes is sexy!

blushing beauty

Apply blush more toward the front of your face, on the apples of your cheeks. Smile and then sweep! It's more youthful and modern than applying blush to the cheek's hollow, which is a bit 1980s and dated.

For special events, prepare your makeup strategy beforehand. Practice your look in a "makeup dress rehearsal"—or book an hour at a makeup studio and have your face professionally done. It's a good idea to have it done a week or so before the Big Event so you know what you are getting and can make any necessary adjustments.

Most important, make sure the makeup you wear is an enhancement and confidence builder. Remember, if it doesn't feel good, take it off!

SHAWN Shawn's singing career puts her onstage— literally. Since the audience is seeing her from afar, her makeup needs to be dramatic, but it's never overdone or heavy. Her eyes are played up with smoky shadow, and her lips and cheeks with natural rosy tones that complement her delicate complexion.

CLAUDIA With her hair pulled softly away from her face and a subtle applica- tion of makeup, Claudia looks fresh and feminine. Note how her lips are emphasized with a bright coral color while her eyes and cheeks are just softly brushed with nude tones.

MARILYN Marilyn is blessed with a beau- tiful olive complexion that needs little enhancement. A sheer lip gloss pays tribute to her full mouth, and taupe shadow and black mascara show off her amazing eyes. A soft peach makes her cheek- bones glow.

TAMARA For evening, Tamara prefers to dramatize her sultry eyes with shimmery shadows in bold strokes, and keep everything else in a neutral color. The effect would not be as strong if her lips were bright red. Tamara's hair is also simple and chic, pulled back into a sleek ponytail.

makeup

TOBI For a working girl on the go like Tobi, makeup has to be simple and clean. Here, pale pink lips, simple, natural eye color, and a single sweep of black mascara, along with a natural blush, create the perfect sophisticated daytime look for this fair-skinned California girl.

CHERYL A glamorous lady requires alluring makeup—but that doesn't mean showy or gaudy. Here Cheryl wears a nude shade of gloss with a slight shimmer. The smoky eye shadows play up her famous blue eyes. A wide swath of pale blush with a subtle glitter adds sparkle to her face without being obvious.

CONSTANCE Constance is so busy she doesn't have time for elaborate makeup when she's off to work. Who does? So she keeps it super-simple with a pale lip color, light blush, and light, bright shadow. All the light colors, applied with a light hand, keep Constance's look very young and pretty.

SANDY The old saying "all a girl needs is lipstick and a smile" could not be proven more accurately than here. Sandy's peach-colored lip gloss and blush combine with a simple barely-there beige shadow to give just the right balance to this redhead's porcelain skin.

"I like my MONEY right where I CAN SEE IT... hanging IN MY CLOSET."

—Carrie Bradshaw, fictional character

CHAPTER 11

putting it together

ORGANIZATION AND SHOPPING

There are two practical aspects of great
personal style that cannot be overlooked:
keeping your wardrobe ordered and making sure your purchases are smart.
Stylish, well-turned-out women are
pulled together at home, too. Great
organization is a characteristic I
notice again and again when
I look into a chic woman's
closet. Furthermore, clothes
cost money. Don't waste your
hard-earned cash buying things
you don't need and neglecting to
replace items you do. Before you purchase new items, you must assess what
you own so you know what's viable and what
you can get rid of. Next, you need to design an
organizational system that lets you find what you
want when you need it. *Then* you can go shopping!

Have Fun in Your Closet

First things first: get rid of wardrobe duds and clothing that holds back your style, such as items that don't fit, are outdated or unflattering, or that you just don't truly love. Send little-worn fashion mistakes to a charity. Basic items such as tops and bottoms that have not been worn in more than a year have got to go.

The exceptions to the one-year rule are unique garments (the sequined bolero, the aqua wrap skirt) and accessories that are useful personality pieces. Try them on to see if there is any validity to them. If so, and you have the room, it is worth saving such items. You'll be surprised how often they come in handy or can be reinvented. I save a lot of unique personality pieces—maybe too many. But I do end up using them. The other exclusion is newish essentials you may have forgotten about and rediscover during Project Clean Out. How many times have you found a T or a pair of pants with the tags still on? Who needs to go shopping when the store is in your bedroom?

It's tough to purge, especially if there is sentiment attached to certain items, or you feel guilty on a financial level. I struggle to get rid of clothes, too. However, you really will feel better once you have cleared out the

don't get hemmed in!

Always keep hem tape on hand. Found in craft and fabric shops, this narrow tape is permeated with fabric glue. When a hem unravels, simply place the tape on the inside of the hem and iron. No sewing required! It's an easy, semipermanent fix.

cobwebs. It's liberating. You'll have a much better idea of what you have and need. And the reward is the opportunity to add the right new things, which makes *you* feel new.

Once you've taken control of your closet and drawers you're ready to get organized. It's easy for well-dressed women to put their look together because everything they need is easy to find. The method of closet planning may differ from woman to woman, but in the end each wardrobe system works. How does a well-thought-out closet help a woman get dressed? She can create new looks or reassemble favorite pairings with ease because garments and accessories are easily located. And organization makes keeping clothes in good repair effortless, so an errant hem or a top that needs cleaning rarely surprises the stylish woman.

I recommend organizing basic clothes by color, from dark to light. If you have room, install three rods in your closet. Divide the closet into two areas with a plank of wood to create an interior wall: one area takes up three-quarters of the closet and the other area, the remaining quarter. In the largest area, install one rod under the top shelf of your closet and the other rod in the middle. Install a rod for dresses under the shelf in the less wide area. On the wider side, use the top rod to hold blouses and shirts, and the bottom rod to hold pants and skirts. Put all your black tops together with dark bottoms underneath and so on. Keep your personality garments in a separate area, if you can—all flowered shirts together, all plaids together, and so on. It is so much easier to put together an outfit if you can put on the basics and then throw in the right personality—the possibilities will seem endless.

Use sturdy wooden hangers to hang clothes whenever you can. Cedar is the best since it absorbs moisture and frustrates moths. Sturdy plastic or fabric-covered padded hangers are the next best things. Oh, and Mommie Dearest was right—wire hangers are the *worst*!

Stack sweaters and Ts in drawers or on open shelving, sorted, again, by color and weight. Never hang knits and jerseys; it ruins the shoulder line and stretches the fabric. If you don't have the room to store warm- and cool-weather items together, make sure off-season clothes are clean (dry-cleaned if appropriate) *before* putting them away in order to discourage moths and other textile-loving creatures from eating holes into them. Place everything in clear plastic storage bins, which further deter moisture, mildew, and bugs. However, don't keep clothing in thin plastic dry cleaning bags—this "bad" plastic traps moisture and helps set in unwanted creases. Acid-free tissue paper placed between folds further maintains stored clothing.

Keep like accessories together. Make room in top bureau drawers or in easily accessed storage boxes for personality jewelry and scarves. The more available these "side dishes" are, the more you will use them. If they are stuffed in the back of a bottom drawer or in the back of the closet, you'll forget about them.

Store shoes and bags in inexpensive clear plastic boxes. Or keep shoes in their original boxes and snap a Polaroid of the shoe and tape it to the front of its box. Stack boxes no more than three high (or you might face an avalanche of shoes when you open your closets). This is a fashion editor's technique, and it works. If you go this route with shoes, line up handbags and totes next to the boxes on the top shelf of the closet or on a shelf at the bottom of the closet.

Caring for clothing is part of keeping organized. After wearing garments, let them hang outside of the closet overnight or for a day so they can air out. This trick cuts

custom fit for pennies

Think you can't afford custom-made clothes? Think again! If you love the style and look of a straight-off-the-rack piece, but it doesn't fit the way it should (or the way you want it to), *buy it*! You can have it altered. Most good dry cleaners have a tailor available who can, for a very reasonable price, change the way a skirt, a jacket, a dress, a blouse, or a pair of pants fits you. Just make sure that the seams are ample enough to work with if the piece you are buying is too small.

down on dry-cleaning bills and wrinkles because airing out clothes freshens them for the next wearing. Make repairs as soon as you can. Open seams, tears, and pulls only get worse over time. Have soiled items cleaned as soon as you possibly can. The longer dirt and food stains sit, the harder they are to remove.

Pull the coming season's clothing out of storage containers a few weeks before you plan to wear them to give them a chance to air out. Hang tops, bottoms, dresses, and coats on a clothesline outside, or at least let them breathe for a couple of days in the house before confining them to your closet.

Shop, Girl!

The world of retail and clothes manufacturing has changed drastically in the past several years. The number of nimble foreign and domestic clothing producers has increased because manufacturing technology and engineering have improved greatly. Even the way we shop for clothes has

in the
bag

When it comes to leather handbags—especially if you are planning on using the same one every weekday and throughout the seasons—finding quality is essential. Here's what to look for:

Quality leather is uniform in texture, grain, and color in all visible and even interior parts of the bag. Even fabric bags should have consistent coloring and fabric. Seams should be straight, and individual stitches should be uniform in size. Zippers should be sturdy and operate smoothly. Clasps should be easy to open and close—but quite secure when they are closed. The same holds true for snaps and magnetic closures. All edges should be carefully finished, with no raggedness. The interior of a bag does not necessarily have to be lined, but if it is, the material should be attached securely to the bag and the fabric should be smooth and sewn with care. Zipper or snap compartments sewn into the lining of a bag should also be sturdy and operate properly (no snagging or struggling to get it closed).

shifted from the mass-market mall to small boutiques, the Internet, and TV. We can find basic clothes and personality pieces in so many different places, it's mind-boggling.

This change is good for the consumer. You can find quality without paying a fortune for it. You can always find a less-expensive version of the latest thing . . . without waiting. Manufacturers have the means and the machinery to respond very quickly to what hot designers and high-end stores are bringing out each season. In fact, big-box retailers, such as Target and Kmart, and discounters, such as H&M, send representatives to the New York fashion shows to see what's hot. And professional trend-watchers tell these stores what's happening in the street. The minute a great look comes off the runway, someone somewhere is making a cheaper version that is just as good and sometimes even better. I don't have a problem with knockoffs. If you can't afford the real thing, why not choose a good copy?

The biggest shift I see is in the manufacture of basic items. Women who are smart shoppers now trade down for basic items instead of up. They have realized they don't need to spend money on such clothes. I'm not sure there are huge quality differences in high- and low-end pants, for example, or if minor production variations even matter so much, if an item is well made overall. If you can find a great pair of black trousers for under $50, why spend $200 or more for the same thing? It doesn't make sense. I visit high-end department stores and see expensive clothes that are shoddily made. And I can go into a big-box retailer and find very decent essentials that are eminently wearable and up-to-date.

Quality can cost more, but not always. High-quantity manufacturers and big department stores have stringent quality controls that boutique designers sometimes lack. The manufacturing standards at Home Shopping Network, for example, are extremely high because customers can't touch the clothes and see for themselves. The layer television creates between the clothing and the customer makes the network strive for quality they can guarantee. The line I design for HSN goes through so much testing that you end up with a very well made item for a great price. The point is you can find quality at every price level, even on TV at two in the morning.

You can't always judge on material alone, either. Maybe it's *supposed* to be a plastic handbag. Maybe the "pleather" pants cost more than the leather ones because the real stuff is poor quality. Touch and hold potential purchases. Discerning quality has a lot to do with instinct and feel. If it looks cheap to you, it probably is. If it feels rich to you, it probably is.

Telltale signs of quality are always found in the details, even in how the label is made. Cheap labels

shoe shopping

Do not buy shoes that don't fit. They won't "grow" as you wear them, and taking a too-small pair of shoes to a cobbler for stretching could ruin them. Ill-fitting shoes not only hurt your feet but also can literally ruin your day. Remember that your entire body is balancing on your feet—be nice to them. Quality counts, too: the best shoes are made entirely of leather, including the sole, the heel, and the lining.

the look:
shopping secrets

- Take your time selecting and trying on clothes.
- Take command of your clothes. Find the tailoring and the fit that are right for *you*, not what others tell you they should be.
- Dress to move. You're not a mannequin. Always make sure you can walk, sit, and glide comfortably in your clothes.
- Focus on clothing strategies that work for your body type.
- Trust your instincts. If it feels wrong, it is. You *know* your authentic style when you see it.
- Double-check impulse purchases—why are you buying it and where will you wear it?
- Break your own rules.

are printed, whereas woven labels signify that the items are better. If a manufacturer puts all the information and care labels underneath the brand label, that's a sign of a lower budget. Higher-quality items have care labels on the side seam or in a location other than in back of the brand label.

On jackets and coats, always look for keyhole buttonholes instead of straight buttonholes. That small, quirky detail is a sign of quality. A four-hole button is better than a two-hole button. Metal zippers are better than plastic ones. A hem that's turned over twice, so the edge is neatly folded, is better than one that is not.

All clothing does not have to be lined to be good, but unlined clothing should have clean, finished French seams, which are seams sewn twice so that no unfinished edges show, or at least have seams finished with overlock stitching. Overlocking stitching on seams or hems should be neat, straight, and tightly sewn. In general, the rule is, the smaller the stitch, the better the quality of the item, unless the stitching is decorative.

When I'm considering a purchase, I also look at how the fabric performs. If it's puckering on the hanger, it will pucker on you. Does the fabric really flatter the style? Maybe the style is right, but the fabric is wrong. I tend to like softer fabrics because they flatter the body more than harder fabrics. Sometimes items made of stiffer fabrics don't fit as well. Does the fabric feel rigid, scratchy, or rough? Or does it feel nice on the hand? How does it look once it's on? Does the fabric drape nicely, if it's a tailored piece? Are the seams straight and do they fall where they should?

When trying on items, sit down and walk around in them. Are you comfortable? Give the fabric a wrinkle test. Scrunch up a corner of fabric in your hands. If it doesn't wrinkle or if the wrinkles fall out right away, it's most likely easy to care for. If the wrinkles stay put, consider the amount of ironing the item will require. Plus, do you want to look like an unmade bed at the end of the day?

"Whoever said money can't buy happiness simply didn't know where to shop."

—**Bo Derek,** actress

A good buy also offers multiplicity of use. A stylish person's wardrobe is filled with pieces that can be worn ten different ways. Versatility is valuable. For example, can a bathing suit cover-up be used as a tunic off the beach? Can a cashmere sweater be worn to work, on the weekends, and with a satin skirt to a dinner party?

Big stores offer variety but can be more difficult to navigate. If you buy a piece of sportswear, you may have to sprint to the bag department and then run to the hosiery aisle to pull it all together. But maybe the store has a personal shopper who can help (in large stores such services are usually free). Small stores have less variety but usually more one-on-one personalized floor help. Either way, make sure return policies are liberal or at least fair.

style diary

Shopping Spree

Reserve half a day for yourself and go to your favorite department store—alone. Sometimes friends can distract you from your purpose. Choose a store that offers the greatest variety of clothing. It's best if you can choose a time when the store is not busy. Once there, pick out several groups of clothing: items that immediately appeal to you; items you wouldn't dare wear (but are really dying to try); and items you *think* aren't for you either because of style, color, or texture. Grab accessories, including shoes. Rally a clerk to help you (but don't let him or her push things on you that you don't like; learn to say, "No, thank you"). Then go and try on everything. Play around; ask other customers what they think. Have fun. Don't feel pressured to buy anything, but if you do find something you absolutely love, buy it. You can always take it back if you change your mind.

Finally, forget about stores that don't respect all women or are not at least polite to the ones their chosen niche doesn't serve. I recently went into a designer's store in Hollywood with a friend who is a perfectly normal size 10. She had to go to the highest size in this store and still, she could *barely* get her arm into the sleeve! That was bad enough, but the finest moment was when the salesgirl sauntered over to us and sniffed, "We really only want to make clothes that fit women with model figures." Oh brother. I said to my friend, "Let's go; there's no reason for us to be here." So we left. If a store doesn't need your business, then don't give it to them. They won't be around for long.

Always shop where you feel comfortable, welcome, and well served. You should take your business and hard-earned dollars to stores where you feel good. The environment is so important to the whole shopping experience.

conclusion

THE PRIVILEGE OF PERSONAL STYLE

I hope this book has inspired you to
give yourself credit for all that you are and
to take a fresh look at your wardrobe. You
now have the fundamental knowledge to
choose silhouettes wisely and the confidence to look beautiful in them.
The clothes are easy to come
by, actually. Trusting yourself,
going with what you love,
and keeping it fun are the
real keys to success in every
aspect of life, including personal
style.   •   Ultimately, you are the
master of your destiny. While there are
many trusted experts out there, they are not
available in those moments when you're alone
and standing in front of your closet. You're able
to rely on yourself, and that is a gift to be prized.

Make getting dressed one of your private pleasures. Enjoy it. In the animal kingdom, the males of the species are the peacocks and the dandies. But in the human world, women have the privilege and ability to strut their style stuff whenever they want. Please don't miss out on this opportunity. Life's too short not to take delight in looking great!

As I have said before, personal style is constantly evolving. It's a reaction to and a reflection of your reality. Your "mission" is to be mindful of your changing world, to give yourself the freedom to play with clothes, and to always stay open to new fashion ideas.

Complete the mission statement certificate below. It's a reminder of what you have gained from working with the ideas and exercises in this book.

mission statement

I am a [SHAPE] _____

who is [PERSONALITY, E.G., GREGARIOUS, THOUGHTFUL, ETC.] _____

_____

_____

and who [HAS THIS OVERALL INTENTION IN HOW I DRESS] _____

_____

_____

I want to step out into the world as a woman who [HAS THESE WISHES,

DESIRES, AND GOALS] _____

_____

_____

(Copy or cut out this certificate and post it on the inside of your closet,
on your dressing room table, or inside your bathroom medicine cabinet.)